The Anglo-Saxon
Avon Valley
Frontier

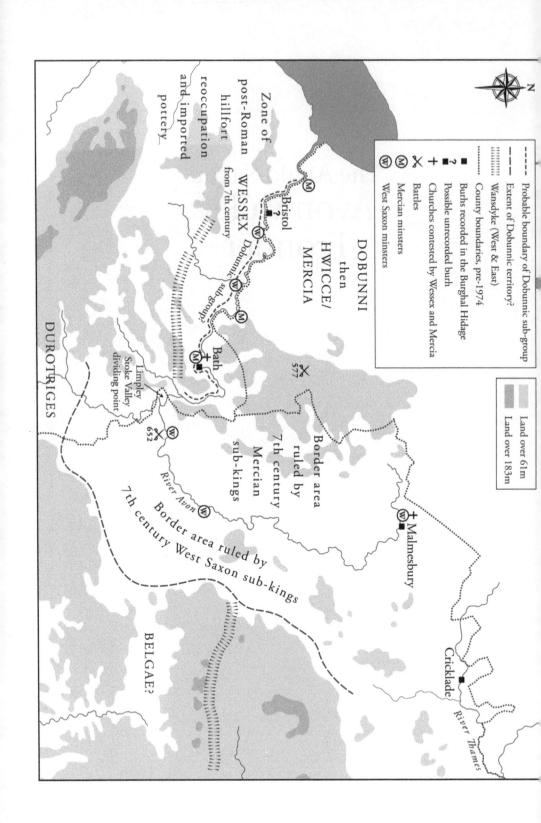

The Anglo-Saxon
Avon Valley Frontier

A RIVER OF TWO HALVES

HANNAH WHITTOCK
AND
MARTYN WHITTOCK

FONTHILL

In memory of the men and women who have lived, worked,
prayed and fought in the valley of the Avon.

Learn more about Fonthill Media. Join our mailing list to
find out about our latest titles and special offers at:
www.fonthillmedia.com

Fonthill Media Limited
www.fonthillmedia.com
office@fonthillmedia.com

First published in the United Kingdom 2014

British Library Cataloguing in Publication Data:
A catalogue record for this book is available from the British Library

ISBN 978-1-78155-282-7

Typeset in 10pt on 13pt Sabon LT Std
Printed and bound by CPI Group (UK) Ltd, Croydon, CR0 4YY

Contents

Acknowledgements

This book is based on research completed within the department of Anglo-Saxon, Norse and Celtic (ASNC) at the University of Cambridge, in 2010, and on work carried out as part of an MPhil within the same department in 2012. In both these pieces of work the internationally renowned Anglo-Saxonist, Professor Simon Keynes, acted as supervisor and his advice and insights assisted both in setting the original aims for each dissertation and in completing that work.

In addition, a number of people provided valuable advice and information which assisted in the research which fed into the two dissertations and related articles (on the Wiltshire county boundary and the annexation of Bath into Wessex) and eventually this book; without them, of course, carrying any responsibility for the interpretations offered by the authors:

Martin Papworth, the National Trust Regional Archaeologist (Wessex Region), provided valuable insights regarding Dobunnic and Durotrigian culture zones. Professor Andrew Reynolds, Professor of Medieval Archaeology, University College London and Dr Bruce Eagles, Visiting Research Fellow, Bournemouth University provided important suggestions during work on the north-western border of Wiltshire. Professor Colin Haselgrove, Professor of Archaeology, University of Leicester, assisted with comments regarding the distribution of Late Iron Age coinage of the Dobunni. Dr Ian Leins, Curator of Iron Age and Roman Coins, Department of Coins and Medals, at the British Museum, offered detailed comments regarding the distribution of Iron Age coins, while interpreting the significance somewhat differently to the view outlined in part of our analysis. Dr Gareth Williams at the British Museum, Dr Martin Allen and Dr Rory Naismith at the Fitzwilliam Museum, Cambridge, and Dr Keith Sugden of the Manchester Museum provided important information regarding the Bath pennies of Edward the Elder. Bruno Barber, Project Officer, Museum of London Archaeology (MOLA) provided information regarding recent work at South Gate, Bath. The overview of current archaeological information concerning the Avon valley region was assisted by: Rod Millard for Bath and North East Somerset, Paul Driscoll for South Gloucestershire and Peter Insole for Bristol. The information (and permission to use photographs) relating to the Budbury Hillfort and Glebe Cottage burials (both in Bradford on Avon) was kindly made available by Roy Canham and Adrian Powell. Peter Bull, of Peter Bull Art Studio, produced the map with a speed and flexibility that was much appreciated.

It goes without saying that responsibility for the interpretations and all errors are our own.

Hannah Whittock and Martyn Whittock.

CHAPTER 1

The Main Evidence Base

In order to carry out an investigation into the history of the Avon valley it is necessary to utilise a wide range of different types of evidence. Since these will be referred to throughout the book it is helpful, at this stage, to explain something about the main sources of evidence that will be referred to. They are outlined below in alphabetical order.

Æthelweard's Chronicle

This is an expanded version of the *Anglo-Saxon Chronicle* (see below). While there is some debate concerning its authorship, the generally accepted view is that it was produced by a senior member of the West Saxon aristocracy. It was probably written between 978 and 988 and most likely towards the end of this date-range. Its author was probably Æthelweard, the *ealdorman* (royal regional representative) whose name appears as a witness on a number of charters (see below) between the years 976 and 998. According to these documents he was the *ealdorman* of the Western Provinces. *Æthelweard's Chronicle* is a Latin translation of a lost version of the Old English *Anglo-Saxon Chronicle* but one that avoids the year-by-year format of the *Anglo-Saxon Chronicle*. In contrast, Æthelweard adopted a running style which gives a continuous narrative, divided into four books. In writing this version, Æthelweard expanded the information to hand with additional material drawn from the writings of the eighth-century Northumbrian monk Bede and from his own West Country sources. As a result we find useful details in Æthelweard's work we do not find in any surviving version of the *Anglo-Saxon Chronicle*. This compensates for Æthelweard's rather impenetrable Latin style! To be fair to Æthelweard, the complex nature of his Latin is testament to the fact a layman (most other writing was done by monks) in the late tenth century could benefit from a comprehensive Latin education and write in a style favoured by a number of contemporary (and equally dense) monastic authors.[1]

Anglo-Saxon Chronicle

This valuable source of evidence was compiled prior to 893 when Asser, King Alfred the Great's biographer, used a version that was already possibly two removes from the original text (and the original was probably written in the 880s). Where it was originally written, why it was written and under whose authority is unknown. Its rapid dissemination may owe something to official royal encouragement but modern scholars are no longer sure that it was an official publication from the court of Alfred. It is written from a West Saxon perspective, but not simply as propaganda for Alfred, as too many opportunities were missed to expand on the king's successes if this had been the intention. Nevertheless, it does give a West Saxon view of Anglo-Saxon history.

In this book, after its first use in each chapter, it is usually just referred to as the *Chronicle*. Once one allows for its West Saxon agenda – except when it clearly incorporates other materials with *their own* specific agendas – it provides a crucial insight into events. Despite the fact its fifth- and sixth-century annals mix myth and oral history, while giving them a spurious chronology which at times is clearly artificial, from the seventh century onwards it offers a valuable (if selective and partial) insight into real events, with a much more persuasive chronology.

An authoritative modern translation of the *Anglo-Saxon Chronicle* is that provided by D. Whitelock and is part of her excellent collection of documents, which also includes a great many other sources for Anglo-Saxon England.[2] However, her translation of the *Chronicle* only extends to 1042 and, as a result, later annals are taken from the translation by D. Whitelock, D. C. Douglas and S. I. Tucker. This gives the full run of annals up to the final one found in the *Anglo-Saxon Chronicle* in 1154.[3] Another accessible translation of the *Chronicle* is that by G. N. Garmonsway.[4]

There are a number of different surviving manuscripts of the *Anglo-Saxon Chronicle* and differences within them reveal the different motivations of – and information available to – different monastic record-keepers as they continued recording and adding to the original document (the so-called 'common stock') they had before them.[5] This is why, at critical points, we refer to distinct manuscripts of the *Chronicle*. The different manuscripts of the *Chronicle* are known by both letters and names. They are:

> *Manuscript A*, the *Parker Chronicle*. This is the oldest surviving version and was almost certainly written in Winchester in the late ninth or very early tenth century. It is rather carelessly written and was probably two removes from the original. It is well informed about Alfred's later Viking wars, the activities of Edward the Elder and royal activities in

the tenth century. Its coverage of events ends at 1001. It was extended at Canterbury in the eleventh or twelfth centuries. It is now kept at Corpus Christi College, Cambridge University.

Manuscript B. It was probably written at Abingdon, although it was at Christ Church Canterbury by 1100. Most of the numbers in its annals are missing, which limits its use in dating events. Its coverage of events ends at 977. It is now in the British Library, London.

Manuscript C, the *Abingdon Chronicle*. It was probably composed in the 1050s and is largely the same as *Manuscripts A* and *B* for earlier events. It contains a set of records called the *Mercian Register* for the years 896-924. These give important insights into events in Mercia and provide a Mercian viewpoint. It provided additional information regarding the reigns of Æthelred II (the Unready) and Cnut. Its eleventh-century writer did not approve of the Godwin family and was possibly associated with the rival noble family of Leofric of Mercia. Its coverage of events ends at 1066. It is now in the British Library, London.

Manuscript D, the *Worcester Chronicle*. This combination of a number of different sources was probably put together in the 1060s. This manuscript was possibly connected with York and Worcester until 1062 and then York until 1069. This is not as unusual as it appears, as Wulfstan II (died 1023) was bishop of Worcester and archbishop of York. It combines the *Mercian Register* with annals of Edward the Elder, has information regarding the reign of Æthelred II (the Unready) and its coverage of events ends at 1079. It is now in the British Library, London.

Manuscript E, the *Laud* or *Peterborough Chronicle*. This was written in East Anglia shortly after *c.* 1116 (its new annals start in 1121 and continue to 1154). It was probably written to replace a manuscript lost in the fire that struck the monastery of Peterborough in 1116. It contains a lot of northern material and is favourably disposed towards the eleventh-century Godwin family. Its coverage of events ends at 1154. It is now in the Bodleian Library, Oxford University.

Manuscript F, the *Bilingual Chronicle*, written in both Old English and Latin. Each entry in Old English is followed by the Latin version. The version the scribe copied is similar to the version used by the scribe in Peterborough who wrote *Manuscript E*, though it seems to have been abridged. It was probably written at Christ Church,

Canterbury between 1100 and 1109. It is now in the British Library, London.

Finally there is *Manuscript G*, a copy of *Manuscript A* but without later material and dating from Winchester in the eleventh century; and *Manuscript H* which dates from the twelfth century and has additional coverage of events for 1113-14.

These different manuscripts sometimes give us distinctly different takes on events and the information can vary from manuscript to manuscript. Within the different manuscripts of the *Chronicle* there are often dislocations in dating which mean the dates given for events can vary in different secondary sources which refer to the same entries. In this exploration we have followed the – corrected – dates given in bold in Whitelock. This makes all our dates consistent.

A number of the key battles and other events that are discussed later on are found in the *Chronicle* and it is therefore a vitally important source of evidence for the history of the Avon valley in the Anglo-Saxon period.

Annals of Wales (*Annales Cambriae*)

The *Annals of Wales* (*Annales Cambriae*) is a Welsh source and written in Latin. It dates from between 960 and 980 and its annals cover a period of over five hundred years. It clearly drew on a wide range of sources of information (Welsh and Irish) and used these to construct a version of the past which suited the agenda of the Welsh (of north Wales) in the late tenth century. Its 'Year 1' was probably AD 447. Because its annals are numbered not dated there is some debate over exactly when events recorded in it occurred. For example, its reference to the first battle of Badon is given as Year LXXII; although a number of experts think this was in 516 or 518, others offer alternative dates. The oldest surviving copy of the *Annals of Wales* is the manuscript known as *Harleian MS 3859*, where it is bound in the same volume with a different source known as the *Historia Brittonum* (which contains Arthurian material) and mixed genealogical lists. It is likely it was influenced by the *Historia Brittonum* (composed *c.* 828) which reflected Welsh patriotism in the face of Anglo-Saxon expansion and the hope of a Welsh political revival. Its relevance to the Avon valley is that it contains two references to the battle of Badon which, we suggest, was probably fought in the vicinity of Bath.

Asser's *Life of King Alfred*

The *Life of King Alfred* is the first biography of an English monarch and was written by Asser, a Welsh monk from St David's, in 893. Earlier, in 885, he was invited by Alfred to join his court, becoming the bishop of Sherborne in 890. This biography recounts Alfred's life from his birth until 893. When writing the *Life*, Asser both translated information he found in the *Anglo-Saxon Chronicle*'s Old English entries into Latin, and expanded upon them with additional information. These expansions are particularly valuable as they give us additional information about many of the key events in Alfred's life and in his wars with the Vikings. It seems clear it was composed for a Welsh audience; Asser was clearly not writing for West Saxons as he carefully explained the local geography of places he discussed and gave Welsh versions for some of the English place names he referred to. The *Life* is divided into six sections. Of these, three are drawn from the *Anglo-Saxon Chronicle* and these are combined with three sections which detail other areas of the king's life. Asser's work is similar to the continental account by Einhard of the *Life of Charlemagne* (written sometime between 817 and 830). This was inspired by an earlier Roman work by Suetonius, called the *Twelve Caesars* (probably written in 121). For a history of the Avon valley, Asser provides important details regarding Burgred's marriage to Æthelswith at Chippenham and the later Viking attack on Chippenham.

Charters

This term covers a large range of Anglo-Saxon documents. These include the royal diplomas which were issued by Anglo-Saxon kings from the seventh century onwards until the Norman Conquest in 1066. These were almost always written in Latin. Most of the surviving collection of Anglo-Saxon charters were records of grants of land or privileges by the king. These were often to a religious house, or to a prominent lay person. While the terms of the charter (diploma) were in Latin the description of the boundary of the estate being granted was usually in Old English. Such documents also included a list of those prominent people who, alongside the king, acted as witnesses to the grant. The collection of charters also includes records of settlements of land-disputes, leases of Church property, and other records of bequests of land and property. Other documents often included under the general heading of 'charters' are wills, which were usually written in Old English.[6] Charters provide important evidence in the exploration of the history of the Avon valley as they give an insight into which Anglo-Saxon kingdom (the Hwicce, Mercia and Wessex) was supporting which Avon valley monastery, the changing balance of power in the region and the political interventions in land ownership along the valley and in its hinterland. Their boundary lists also provide information about road networks and land-use.[7]

Coinage

The origins of coinage in Britain is intimately connected with the activities of powerful political systems operating on the other side of the Channel in continental Europe. British Late Iron Age coins were strongly influenced by coins made by Continental tribes who were themselves copying coins produced in Greece and the Greek Empire from the fourth century BC. On these early Greek coins the head of Apollo was depicted wearing a laurel wreath; in the copies this became deconstructed into a stylised series of pellets and crescents on the obverse (head-side) of the coin. The Greek coins also carried a two-horse chariot on the reverse; in the copies this often became little more than a combination of disjointed crescents.[8] These coins first appear as imports into Britain in the late second or early first century BC and were then copied by British rulers. As Roman power increased in Gaul, Roman coins with Latin titles increasingly influenced these emerging British coins. The relevance to the Avon valley is that different British Late Iron Age tribal groups and sub-groups minted these coins using different decorative motifs and the distribution pattern of these coin finds may indicate the political, as well as economic, spheres of influence of these tribes. This remains a matter of debate amongst numismatists but is important when exploring the use of the river Avon as a boundary in the Late Iron Age.

With the end of Roman rule, in the early fifth century, coinage ceased in Britain. The coinage system had been a direct by-product of imperial rule and by the 430s the end of coin use was final. Where coins are found in later fifth-century contexts they were almost certainly used as bullion (metal valued by weight), not as coins. Where coins are found on Anglo-Saxon sites they do not show the last kinds issued but rather issues across the Roman period. This suggests they turned up in fields or on old sites, and were recycled as jewellery, or bullion. Imports of the occasional Byzantine bronze and copper coins occurred in the sixth century; probably as a result of trade and/or diplomatic missions from the Eastern Roman Empire. These end after the early seventh century, probably as a result of the dislocation of the Byzantine economy as a result of wars in the Middle East which distracted the attention of the Eastern Roman emperors. Gold coins then do not appear again in England until the 650s; followed by silver proto-pennies (often called *sceattas* by modern numismatists). These eventually gave way to a larger, broader coin which copied ones being produced across the Channel in Francia and which would come to be known as pennies. This development was given a boost when the Mercian king, Offa, adopted the new penny coinage, which had started in Kent.

Coins can tell us a great deal about the growth of the economy and the role of kings. The iconography of coins can convey political and religious messages, while royal titles communicate royal power and propaganda. The places where coins were minted reveal something of the geography of power and the development of towns. With regard to the Avon valley, this is particularly revealing concerning the relationship between Mercia and Wessex. For example there seems to have been some kind of monetary union between the two kingdoms *c*. 867 and *c*. 875. The so-called 'Two Emperors' coinage of Alfred the Great of Wessex and Coenwulf II of Mercia may have been chosen for its political significance. These coins also show 'greater interaction between the kings' than on similar Roman coins and this suggests 'an intentional message in the reworking of the image'.[9] It is all the more revealing therefore when, in the early tenth century, we find West Saxon coins being minted in a Mercian town (Bath) and carrying a royal title that proclaims West Saxon monarchy. Clearly, something politically significant had occurred in the Avon valley prior to this, which had caused a major shift in the balance of power at Bath.

Dream of Rhonabwy (*Breuddwyd Rhonabwy*)

This Welsh mythological document, which sets itself in the context of the politics of the rule of Madog of Powys (died 1160), looks back to the battle of Badon or Baddon, (a real event) and names Arthur's rival as Owain son of Urien of Rheged, a kingdom centred on the Solway Firth but whose lands stretched over north-western England and into Yorkshire. These last two were historic rulers in the 'Old North' (northern Britain before the Anglo-Saxon conquests) in the sixth century. This is in contrast to the semi-mythical (possible wholly-mythical) Arthur. Whilst Owain has been very much transmuted into a mythical character, he was originally a real warrior. Similarly, another enemy is Osla *Gyllellfawr* (big-knife). Described as leader of the Saxon armies at Badon, he may have represented a garbled version of the name of the eighth-century Mercian ruler, Offa.[10] In the dream itself, Rhonabwy was guided by a character named Iddog who was responsible for causing the battle of Camlan in which Arthur was killed. However, the time in the story was then telescoped and the reader finds the focus has shifted to just before the battle of Badon, an earlier battle; the location of which was near the river Severn. This is why it has relevance to the history of the Avon valley as it corroborates the Welsh medieval tradition that the battle of Badon was fought in the vicinity of Bath.

Geoffrey of Monmouth's *History of the Kings of Britain* (*Historia Regum Britanniae*)

Written, *c.* 1136, by a member of the Norman elite of the Welsh border country, who went on to become the bishop of St Asaph and who died in 1154, this was a medieval best-seller. This is revealed in the fact that 186 manuscripts of the *Historia* have survived; of which 48 are complete manuscripts, and two date from as early as the twelfth century. It purports to tell a history of Britain from the origin of Britain in the activities of Brut, the great grandson of Acheaus in 1100 BC, to the final triumph of the Saxons and the death of the Welsh ruler, Cadwallader in 689. It is most famous for its reworking of earlier myths (Welsh and Breton) about King Arthur and its presenting of these in a dramatic story than has influenced Arthurian literature ever since. It is certainly not a work of history but of literature and should be read as historical-fiction at best. Its relevance to the Avon valley story lies in Geoffrey's record of the tradition that the battle of Badon was fought outside Bath. However, Geoffrey on his own would not be sufficiently reliable for arguing this.

Gildas' *The Ruin and Conquest of Britain* (*De Excidio et Conquestu Britanniae*)

Probably writing in the 540s, the British writer, Gildas, has left us with a vital but hard to disentangle account of the fifth-century arrival of the Anglo-Saxons and the loss of eastern Britain to these invaders. Whilst his account is short on names, dates and geography, his account of the building of defensive dykes may be a reference to earthworks such as Wansdyke, as well as a garbled echo of traditions concerning the Roman construction of Hadrian's Wall.

History of the Britons (*Historia Brittonum*)

The Latin *History of the Britons* (*Historia Brittonum*), often attributed to a compiler named Nennius, was written *c.* 828, early in the reign of Merfyn of Gwynedd. Its aim was to counter the very negative view of the Welsh as condemned by God for their sins, which had been presented by the sixth-century British writer, Gildas, and was later taken up and used by Bede, the eighth-century Anglo-Saxon writer. In place of this downbeat view of the Welsh, the deeds of the heroic figure of Arthur were described in the *History of the Britons* and he was credited with a series of twelve battles. In this he was presented as a new Joshua – the warrior leader of Israel in the Old Testament – and this heroic Arthur led God's people (the Christian Welsh) in their successful resistance to the pagan Anglo-Saxons. Its importance to the Avon valley story lies in an appendix called *The Wonders of Britain (de mirabilibus Britanniae)* which describes an amazing natural feature as 'the Baths of Badon' and corroborates the Welsh medieval tradition that the battle of Badon was fought in the vicinity of Bath.

Place Names

The majority of the place names on the modern map of the Avon valley region originated in Old English (the language of the Anglo-Saxons); although a small number were originally formed from British (the ancestor of modern Welsh). These place names are a valuable indicator of land-use and settlement patterns. Consequently, they give us an insight into the wooded nature of the Limpley Stoke Valley and its environs. They also offer clues regarding the survival of British-speaking communities in the area, despite the Anglo-Saxon takeover in the seventh century. A name such as Wansdyke also provides additional information when trying to understand this enigmatic earthwork. Some place names, such as Bedminster, point towards Church estates along the valley which are discernible in other forms of evidence such as charters, chronicles and later medieval hierarchies of churches and ecclesiastical privileges.

Pottery

From the Neolithic (New Stone Age) period (*c.* 4000 BC), onwards, pottery has played an important part in the lives of people living in Britain and has provided a valuable source of information to archaeologists. While experts disagree over the cultural and political significance of the distribution patterns of different ceramic types and styles, the fact that these existed clearly communicates something about tribal identities as well as economics and trade patterns. In the Late Iron Age the distribution of some pottery styles reinforces the suggestion – based on coin distribution patterns – that tribal boundaries may be discerned in the vicinity of the river Avon. This ceases to be significant in the Roman period (*c.* 43–410) since political unity and industrial-scale ceramic production meant that pottery was distributed across a far wider area than before. However, with the collapse of Roman rule in the early fifth century, pottery distribution patterns play a major part in charting the role of the river Avon as a cultural (and possibly political) boundary. The end of commercial Roman-era pottery manufacture meant that friable, organic-tempered pottery became the dominant kind of ceramic used in the sub- and post-Roman communities in the Avon valley region. However, the additional presence of pottery of Mediterranean origin south of the 'western Avon' indicates that the river constituted some form of cultural boundary. By the time that the area passed under Anglo-Saxon dominance their distinctive pottery (used for example in Anglo-Saxon cremation cemeteries further east) had ceased to be used and thereafter pottery ceases to be such a useful diagnostic tool.

Sites and Monuments

The sites and monuments relevant to a study of the Avon valley range from the remains at Roman Bath (*Aquae Sulis*) indicating the transition to a sub-Roman kingdom, to burial sites that indicate the cultural allegiances of those buried there (although these are few in number). Others, such as the Wansdyke earthwork, offer a tangible clue concerning political frontiers in the fifth century, following the end of Roman rule. Still others, such as the high status site at Cowage Farm, south-west of Malmesbury, provide evidence for royal halls that were built in this sensitive strategic area. Ecclesiastical sites – known from written records – can also be deduced from architectural fragments discovered in places such as Bath and Keynsham.

William of Malmesbury, *Deeds of the Kings of the English* (*Gesta regum Anglorum*)

This source, written *c.* 1125, contains letters, plus legends and stories current in the twelfth century, along with Malmesbury traditions on the subject of King Athelstan. Given this king's association with the Avon valley monastery of Malmesbury, this makes it a particularly valuable source of information. In fact, we are especially indebted to William of Malmesbury for much of our knowledge regarding Athelstan. Without the work of this twelfth-century monastic historian we would know very little about this major player in the tenth-century phase of the Viking Wars. However, despite writing two centuries after Athelstan, William clearly had access to much earlier evidence, including traditions preserved at Malmesbury (Athelstan's burial place).

CHAPTER 2

From the Late Iron Age to Late Roman Britain: Order Imposed or Crisis Deferred?

This chapter explores the evidence for *civitas* boundaries in the Roman period in the Avon valley region and relates them to evidence for Late Iron Age political units in the area. A *civitas* was a Roman local government area based on British tribal groups which had come into existence before the start of Roman rule in AD 43. The evidence strongly suggests that, while Roman rule saw some major changes to local tribal boundaries, the imperial *civitas* boundaries were clearly based on ones which originally dated from the Late Iron Age (the modern label used to describe the pre-Roman culture of Britain). This provides a foundation for the later analysis of political and cultural boundaries in the Anglo-Saxon period because it is clear these earlier boundaries continued to influence the frontiers which emerged after the end of Roman rule in Britain *c.* 410. This analysis will also assess the impact of Roman administrative decisions on these boundaries and the evidence that these 'arrangements' were challenged at the end of imperial rule.

The River in Question: the 'Bristol Avon'

The river Avon rises on the edge of Badminton Park (Gloucestershire), at Cherry Orchard, a point just within the north-western boundary of Wiltshire. This is particularly appropriate given its importance in the history of boundaries and frontiers along its route. As with all rivers, it is difficult to decide its ultimate start, since so high on its course it relies on a number of feeder-streams to form a recognisable river. A more dramatic point at which the river's journey could be said to start is at the appropriately named Crow Down Springs, west of Sherston (Wiltshire). From here it flows to meet the Badminton Park tributary on the western outskirts of Sherston and flows on as the 'Sherston Avon'. From Sherston, the river first drains eastwards and then southwards in a wide curve through Wiltshire. At Malmesbury, it joins up with its first major tributary, the 'Tetbury Avon', which rises just north of Tetbury, in Gloucestershire. From this point onwards it is known simply as the Avon or the 'Bristol Avon'. After the two tributary rivers merge at Malmesbury, the Avon then turns south-east away from the Cotswolds and then south into the clayland of the Dauntsey Vale, until it reaches Chippenham. The wide river valley in this section of the river's course is now known as the Avon Vale. The river flows on to Melksham, via Lacock, then turns north-west through Bradford on Avon, with a steep river-cliff on its northern bank.

Beyond Bradford on Avon, the river cuts through the Limpley Stoke Valley where, at points, the river's course is dramatic and gorge-like. High land rises away from the river on either bank: to the north lies the Cotswolds and to the south the rising land soon joins the eastern end of the Mendip Hills. As a result, the river Avon has two distinct sections: one east of Bath and the Limpley Stoke Valley; one west of Bath. This makes it something of a 'river of two halves' and this, as we shall see, is more than a geographical feature, for this distinction underpins millennia of the contrasting character of the river's use as a frontier.

After Bath the river flows westward to Keynsham, skirting Saltford, and then reaches Bristol. The course of the river through Bristol is marked by the so-called Floating Harbour which maintains the level of the river, while the true tidal nature of the Avon at this point in its course is still seen in the New Cut, which was dug between 1804 and 1809. The original course of the Avon through the centre of the city and the Floating Harbour takes one to the very heart and origins of Bristol (and indeed its name – the 'bridge-place' over the Avon) which will be explored towards the end of this history of the Avon valley in the Anglo-Saxon period. After Bristol, the river cuts through the high limestone ridge at Clifton Gorge and eventually joins the Severn estuary at Avonmouth.

The river name itself is first recorded, in the form *Abon*, in a charter purportedly dating from 688 and the same form is found in the late ninth-century writings of the Welsh bishop Asser, who was a member of the West Saxon court of King Alfred. The name is derived from a British form *abona*, meaning 'river' and the word later developed into the Welsh form *afon*. From this it developed into the modern 'Avon'.[1] There are, in total, four rivers in England named Avon. There is some debate over whether the original British name was the actual name of the river or was, instead, a name for rivers generally. For example, the modern name of the river flowing through Cardiff is, in Welsh, the *afon Taf* (river Taff). However, the fact the Roman settlement at Sea Mills, on the crossing-point of the river Severn, was named *Abona* indicates it took its name from the river and so suggests this was the actual name of the river itself. This particular place name itself is recorded in the *Antonine Itinerary* as *Abone* and in the *Ravenna Cosmography* it appears in the corrupt form *Punctuobice*. It is very likely this is a garbled form of either *Portu Abone* or *Portum Abonae*, and meant 'port of/at Avon'.[2] The *Antonine Itinerary* (full name the *Itinerarium Provinciarum Antonini Augusti*) is a Roman document which contains 225 routes along the roads of the Roman Empire. It is not of one date. One part, at least, dates from the mid third century while other parts may date from the early second century and it may have acquired its present form in the early fourth century. The *Ravenna Cosmography* was compiled *c.* 700 at Ravenna, Italy, and lists about 5,000 place names of the old Empire and beyond. It is, though, very disorganised; in places it confuses towns with rivers and *vice versa* and lists settlements large and small as a *civitas*, without any attempt to differentiate either their size or their significance.

The Avon was an important river from the pre-Roman period until the Norman Conquest and often appears to have acted as a frontier. In order to discuss the extent to which the Avon valley was a frontier region it is necessary to compare the literary evidence from the Roman and early medieval sources with the archaeological evidence and also to take into account charters which form such an important source of evidence in the Anglo-Saxon period (see Chapter 1). It is necessary to bring together this wide range of evidence from different disciplines in order to create a full picture of the fluctuating history of the Avon and to explain both the patterns and anomalies in its role as a frontier. There are indeed both patterns and anomalies; but both of these features point to something of the history of the river as a boundary. First, it must be explained why the river *should* be examined as a possible frontier. As we shall shortly see there are very good reasons for looking at rivers as frontiers and so the question of how the river Avon fulfilled this role is a very reasonable one to ask.

Rivers as Anglo-Saxon Frontiers

It is certainly clear river systems were used, in a number of significant and influential examples, as boundaries in Anglo-Saxon England. This is apparent from the available written evidence. The Northumbrian churchman, Bede, writing in the 730s,[3] makes it clear the river Humber was a long-lasting political boundary between the Northumbrians and their southern neighbours.[4] Bede reminds us it formed 'the boundary between the north and south Angles'.[5] In his day this had become the frontier between Northumbria and its bitter rival the Mercians since, by the early eighth century, the Mercians had long-since annexed the once-independent kingdom of Lindsey in Lincolnshire. Bede was well aware of the frontier-role of rivers for he also specifically describes the kingdom of the East Saxons (Essex) as being 'separated from Kent by the river Thames'.[6] London was regarded as an East Saxon city even when Essex was dominated by the king of Kent. Although the king of Kent was influential in the city at this time, it is clear he was operating over the border and demonstrating the power which allowed him to interfere in the territory of a rival kingdom. This river-boundary was so well established that any extension of political power south of it was noteworthy. Consequently, the sub-kingdom of Surrey carried a name which illustrates this; it was the '*Suþrige*', the 'southern district', when it was first recorded in 722 in the *Anglo-Saxon Chronicle*.[7]

This use of rivers as boundaries appeared in a number of Anglo-Saxon regions. The patterns of Anglo-Saxon artefact distribution in East Anglia, separated by the rivers Lark and Gipping, is very similar to artefact distribution of the pre-Roman tribe of the Iceni in the Late Iron Age.[8] What this means is that in the Anglo-Saxon period (as earlier in the Late Iron Age) there were different cultural groups living either side of these rivers and signalling their contrasting identities through different ethnic identifiers such as different kinds of pottery and metalwork. As we shall see, this foreshadows a very similar pattern that will be explored with regard to the river Avon.

A similar use of rivers as frontiers can be seen from the earliest (semi-legendary) accounts of the origins of the Anglo-Saxon kingdoms, right through to the end of Anglo-Saxon England in the mid-eleventh century. The *Anglo-Saxon Chronicle* makes a number of very specific references to rivers marking the limits of early kingdoms in the fifth to seventh centuries. Its annal for 485 records how the South Saxon king, 'Ælle fought against the Britons near the bank of [a river called] *Mearcredesburna*'.[9] This river name has not survived into modern use but it seems that originally it meant something like 'the stream of the agreed frontier'.[10] One could hardly wish for more compelling evidence to show how battles and boundaries were often located on rivers in the Anglo-Saxon period. There is every likelihood this was also true in earlier periods of history since the frequent discoveries of Bronze Age and Iron Age military gear in rivers suggests these locations were probably chosen because they were liminal places, on the edges of communities (as well as being considered the appropriate locations of the homes of gods and goddesses and entrances to the Otherworld). This is in contrast to their other function as major route-ways which also united groups living on either bank. Clearly, a river had the curious capacity to unite communities even as it was dividing them.

Returning to the Anglo-Saxon period, another annal in the *Anglo-Saxon Chronicle* records how, in 658, the West Saxon king, Cenwealh, defeated the Britons and consequently put them 'to flight as far as the [river] Parret'.[11] Yet another annal – that for 716, in manuscript C of the *Chronicle* – includes a reference to the death of Osred, a Northumbrian king. But what is interesting is that this annal is extended, in Manuscripts D and E of the *Chronicle*, with the words 'south of the border'.[12] This is almost certainly a reference to the river Humber again, in a way that would have been immediately familiar to Bede.

The use of rivers as boundaries continued throughout the Anglo-Saxon period. During the Viking Wars the *Alfred-Guthrum Treaty*, of the 880s, was agreed between Alfred of Wessex and Guthrum, the Viking leader who had earlier failed to capture Alfred in 878 and had himself been defeated and then had settled for the position of king of a Viking-dominated East Anglia. In this treaty the two leaders finally agreed their relative spheres of influence and, in defining the interface between their two rival kingdoms, famously described it as being: 'First about our boundaries [*landgemæra*]: up the Thames, and then up the Lea, and along the Lea to its source, then straight to Bedford, then up the Ouse to Watling Street'.[13] No fewer than four of the boundaries are along rivers. Clearly, for men who were both experienced warriors and rulers the function of rivers as boundaries was assumed. Similarly, in 927, a later West Saxon king – Athelstan –fixed his border with the West Welsh (that is the Cornish) on the river Tamar. It remains the boundary of Cornwall to this day. In the same period he also established his border with the Welsh at the river Wye.[14]

This boundary function of rivers outlived the end of Anglo-Saxon England in 1066. This is clear from the Norman document *Domesday Book* (1086). This reveals that, as late as the 1080s, the rivers Tees and Ribble still marked the northern extent of the local government taxation system which was characteristic of England to the south. Clearly, a cultural, political and administrative boundary could and often was fixed along the course of a river. As if this example were not proof enough, Norman records indicate that in the north-west, the shire structure (found elsewhere in England) itself ceased and the *Domesday* commissioners described the area as '*Inter Ripam et Mersham*' ('Between the Ribble and the Mersey'). In this case the rivers in question represented a recognisable English region, but one whose local government system was unlike that of other English regions.[15] The key point though is it was rivers that were used to demarcate this distinctive area.

What all this demonstrates is that even a limited examination of the evidence reveals it was common for rivers to function as boundaries in the Anglo-Saxon period. It is also clear from the examples cited above that the frequent and early way in which rivers functioned in this fashion clearly indicates this was not an invention of the Anglo-Saxon period (*c.* 410–1066). The examples make a lot more sense if we assume they were well established in this role by the fifth and sixth centuries and that this function had existed before (indeed well before) the end of Roman rule in the early fifth century. The lack of comparable documentary evidence for the Roman and Iron Age periods, compared with the Anglo-Saxon period, means this is more difficult to demonstrate for these earlier times. However, other evidence (most notably the distribution of archaeological artefacts) can be used to fill something of this evidence vacuum. Consequently, it seems clear many Anglo-Saxon boundaries were simply the latest manifestation of a much older historical tradition. This was certainly the case with regard to the Bristol Avon.

As a result it is appropriate to consider how the Avon functioned in this regard. It is a reasonable assumption it might have possessed this frontier characteristic and, as we shall see, there is a convincing array of evidence which proves this was indeed the case. The examination of the river Avon that follows reveals that it too had a boundary function, although the situation in this case was complex and was one that had a clearly anomalous character. This anomaly will be one of the consistent strands which runs through over two millennia of history.

One of the striking characteristics of the eastern course of the Avon is that kingdom, shire and diocesan (Church) boundaries ignore the course of the river. However, this is not the case with regard to boundaries and their relationship with the course of the river west of the Limpley Stoke Valley. This raises the obvious question as to why this difference should have occurred? We will soon see this anomaly is first recognisable in the Late Iron Age; this pattern continued to influence boundaries under Roman rule and then throughout the Anglo-Saxon period. These contrasting patterns continue to influence modern boundaries in the twenty-first century.

The 'Western Avon' as a Frontier in the Late Iron Age

In the Late Iron Age and continuing into the Roman period, the river Avon does not appear to have been a frontier along its entire length. This complex nature of the river can be deduced from a scattering of evidence, which in combination presents us with a convincing picture of arrangements (albeit with some major questions unanswered). In order to make sense of this examination of the evidence, we will call the Avon west of the Limpley Stoke Valley the 'western Avon' and its course east of this point the 'eastern Avon'. These names though are invented for this study in order to avoid confusion and they will not be found on any map.

By mapping the distribution of Late Iron Age coinage it is possible to gain a rough idea of the pre-Roman tribal boundaries in Britain. In this, the key tribal groups in question are those known to modern historians and archaeologists as the Dobunni, the Durotriges, and the Belgae. While historians and archaeologists continue to argue about how cohesive these Iron Age tribal areas were, evidence from Roman sources indicates the Dobunni were a powerful tribe centred on what we now call Gloucestershire; the heartland of the Durotriges appears to have been in Dorset, southern

Somerset and south-western Wiltshire; and the Belgae had their tribal centre in the vicinity of what is now Winchester. All of these tribes minted coins in the period before the Roman conquest of AD 43, in imitation of the imperial superpower which dominated lands beyond the Channel. While the earliest coins carried no inscriptions, later ones carried the names of the rulers who ordered their minting. Some of these rulers are known from Roman accounts of still-independent Britain but most are known only from these coins. The growing numbers of such coins has greatly added to the names of rulers known from Late Iron Age Britain and it seems clear the political landscape must have been extremely complex with many local rulers, although some of these may have operated as sub-kings under a more powerful overlord. The coins themselves carry a range of different designs. Those bearing pictures of horses clearly copied Greek designs that had become less like the original, the further time and distance separated these copies from the original minting of the Greek coins. The degree of similarity to the original coins varied widely. In some examples we can still see a juxtaposition of horse and wheels that once denoted a chariot. In other cases the component parts have become so deconstructed that, were it not for the existence of the original coins, we might struggle to make sense of the swirling curves, arcs and circles. Other coins carried images of ears of corn and of faces (whether the latter represented rulers or divinities is difficult to decide). It is possible to view images of these coins on the website of the Portable Antiquities Scheme.[16]

The coins relevant to mapping the Late Iron Age political landscape of the Avon valley (as we shall shortly see) are those minted by rulers named: Bodvoc, Corio and Catti. Coins of Bodvoc carry a deconstructed horse and chariot on the reverse (of the type just mentioned) and on the obverse (head-side), sometimes just his name and sometimes a portrait and his name. The portrait is sometimes bearded and sometimes clean-shaven. The large number of coins of Corio usually carry an image of an ear of wheat (or possibly a tree) on the obverse, occasionally just the name; and the common horse and chariot image on the reverse. The less common coins of Catti carry the popular horse and chariot motif on the reverse and the ear of wheat/tree on the obverse. There may be a connection between the possible tree image and the name of the later Roman town of *Corinium Dobunnorum* (modern Cirencester), since the name '*Corinium*' may have been derived from a British word meaning 'medlar-tree', which was related to the later Welsh word *ceri*, used for this tree. By the ninth century Cirencester was known in Old Welsh as *Cairceri* to the Welsh bishop, Asser in his *Life of King Alfred* and as *Cair Ceri* in the *History of the Britons (Historia Brittonum)*. This may therefore have been a kind of tribal symbol associated with the Dobunni. [17] What is definite though is the fact that, apart from the names on their coins, we know nothing about these British rulers from the Iron Age. It has been suggested that the place name *Durocornovium*, used for the Roman road-side settlement located at Lower Wanborough, near Swindon, may hide a corrupted form of the name Corio,[18] but this is far from certain.

While these coins show us where they were used, lost or deposited rather than who was politically in control at that point in the landscape, their distribution nevertheless reveals the interplay of influences between different competing Iron Age tribal authorities. At the very least, they give us a broad-brush picture of which group/ruler was dominant where; and they reveal where it was acceptable to trade or distribute coins carrying particular names and symbols that must have communicated political and ethnic messages. As the distribution patterns reduce we are clearly seeing something indicative of the reduction of cultural influence. There is though no absolute dividing point in such distributions and scattered coins can be found in areas otherwise characterised by the coins minted by a different authority. This, though, is not surprising as the vagaries of trade and the bullion value of these silver coins would have meant that there would not have been absolute demarcation points. The pattern that does emerge though is intriguing.

The distribution of coinage assumed to be Dobunnic demonstrates the Bath area and the Avon valley here were firmly within this tribal grouping.[19] Dobunnic territory appears to have straddled the Avon both to the west and east of Bath; running down to the Mendips in the south-west and in the south-east to a frontier with the Durotriges in the vicinity of the river Wylye and Salisbury Plain.[20]

However, despite this, the Avon valley west of Bath (and the Limpley Stoke Valley) may still have constituted a kind of border *within* Dobunnic territory. There are different styles of pottery used to the north and south of the 'western Avon' and – while coins carrying the name Corio are found north and south of the river – coins with the name of Bodvoc are almost exclusively found to the north[21] and north-east of the Avon.[22] It is though apparent that few coins carrying the name Corio are found in the area around Cirencester (the same also applies to coins of Catti), whereas the Bodvoc-issues show a noticeable concentration around Cirencester and are also found to the north-east of this location.[23] There is also some similarity between the distribution of these Bodvoc coins and another type of coinage known as 'Western IJ'.[24] The idea that this pattern of finds represents political areas of influence has been questioned by some experts,[25] who are doubtful that these coins can be used to reveal the extent of tribal territories.[26] However, despite these concerns, others who have studied the distribution have felt inclined to argue that political areas of influence may indeed have led to this distribution. In which case, the 'western Avon' was probably an internal boundary separating a sub-unit of the Dobunni from the main area of Dobunnic culture.[27] Later evidence corroborates this latter interpretation that there was something distinctive about the area south of the river Avon. The close correlation between the suggested northern river border of this sub-unit of the Dobunni and the later West Wansdyke indicates that there was indeed something distinctive about the British communities living south of the river Avon which set them somewhat apart from the British communities living north of the river. Exactly what this meant with regard to politics, power and ethnicity is now lost to us. Nevertheless, what does seem clear is that, within the large tribal area of the Dobunni, those south of the river had a peculiar sense of their own particular identity. In the fifth century AD this exploded into a fierce rivalry that has left a dramatic mark on the landscape which survives to present times; but more on this later.

The 'Western Avon' under Roman Rule

How this rather complex Late Iron Age situation affected political arrangements in the Roman period is more difficult to discern since the evidence for *civitas* boundaries is slight and most mappings of these boundaries are highly conjectural. The Latin term *civitas* (plural *civitates*) was used in the period of Roman rule to describe a local government area within the Roman Empire which was based on the tribal lands of a tribe incorporated into the Empire. The word appears in Roman inscriptions which indicate these local government areas played an important part in imperial administration. For example, an inscription found far to the north on Hadrian's Wall reads: '*c. Durtrg endinesis*'. Based on the fairly consistent way in which words were abbreviated on such monuments, alongside other inscriptions and scattered references, this almost certainly should be read as: '*c(ivitas) Dur(o)tr(i)g(um) (L)endin(i)e(n)sis*'[28] and means 'the tribal group of the Durotriges of Lendiniae built this' and refers to labourers sent north from the Roman town at what is now Ilchester (Somerset). Two of the three tribal groups whose borders are relevant to the river Avon had their names (and their tribal centres) preserved in the place names of important Roman towns. So, the Dobunni gave their name to *Corinium Dobunnorum* (modern Cirencester),[29] and the Belgae to *Venta Belgarum* (modern Winchester).[30] The Durotriges did not have a place name which cited the tribal name; probably because the tribal administration was split between what is now Dorchester (Dorset) and Ilchester (Somerset), but the inscription from Hadrian's Wall indicates the existence of a local government area based on the tribe and this is corroborated by other evidence.

In some modern reconstructions of the Roman *civitas* boundaries, the Avon loses all boundary functions along its entire course, with the territory of the Dobunni (with its *civitas* capital at *Corinium*/Cirencester) stretching as far south as the Mendips and south-eastward onto Salisbury Plain.[31] A different suggestion is that, while northern Somerset may have still been under the control of the Dobunni, Bath may have been administered by the Belgae.[32] In these scenarios, neither the Dobunni nor the Belgae would have regarded the river Avon as a boundary. However, if Dobunnic territory did in fact reach the Mendips this may have involved a reassertion of control over that sub-unit of Dobunnic territory which appears to lie behind the pre-Roman distribution of the coins of Bodvoc/Corio/Catti. In such a scenario the 'western Avon' may still have been a recognised – if temporarily suspended – boundary of a sub-group of the Dobunni which was temporarily overridden by imperial Roman arrangements which emphasised the unity of what we might call 'Greater Dobunnic' territory as far south as the Mendips. It looks as if the later building of West Wansdyke was a reaction against this imperial incorporation. In contrast, the claim that the Belgae controlled Bath strongly suggests the 'eastern Avon' was ignored as a boundary in the period of Roman rule as it had earlier been in the Late Iron Age. However, the tribal group in question had dramatically changed.

Fishing in Troubled Waters… the 'Eastern Avon' under Roman Rule

East of the Limpley Stoke Valley, the 'eastern (Wiltshire) Avon' does not appear to have had a frontier role in the Late Iron Age. The territory of the Dobunni met that of the Durotriges near the source of the river Wylye,[33] and the Dobunni had a border with the Belgae in the vicinity of Salisbury Plain.[34] This changed under Roman rule, as we shall shortly see, as Belgic power was pushed further to the west to include Bath.

Before we examine that development there is one issue that needs to be addressed. It has recently been suggested that the coins usually described as being produced by the 'Dobunni' were actually issued by rulers of independent little tribal sub-groups. It is further argued, these were not formed into a political unit (called in Latin the *Civitas Dobunnorum*) until the Roman period. This occurred as a direct result of Roman intervention in British tribal politics.[35] This is a thought-provoking suggestion but, even if correct, the evidence still suggests that a pre-Roman cultural frontier of some kind lay near the upper-Wylye and the western edge of Salisbury Plain. This is because the plotting of the distribution of find-spots of the, so-called, 'Western coinage',[36] (regarded as Dobunnic by a number of other historians) shows that south and south-east of this line finds drop away dramatically. In short, it is clear that the influence of a pre-Roman Cotswolds-based culture (represented in some form through the 'Western Coinage') extended well to the south-east of the course of the 'eastern Avon'. This was not to last.

The extent of this 'Dobunnic' political/cultural influence was curtailed under Roman rule because Bath, in the Roman period, was included in Belgic territory. This evidence is found in Ptolemy's *Geography*, which was written around the year 150. He identified Bath by the name *Aquae Calidae* (hot springs) and described it as a *polis* (city) of the Belgae.[37] Incidentally, he identified it using the Greek word *polis*, rather than the Latin word *civitas* because he came from the eastern – Greek speaking – part of the Roman Empire. He also used the word *polis* very loosely to cover settlements that varied greatly in size.

Claudius Ptolemy was an astronomer and mathematician who lived in the second century AD in Alexandria (modern Egypt). His most famous writings are the *Almagest*, an astronomical textbook which laid the foundations of trigonometry, an astrological work called the *Tetrabiblos* and the *Geography*. This latter book consisted of an atlas of the known world of his day consisting of maps and text. While his maps have disappeared, it has proved possible (if difficult and controversial) to reconstruct them from other information in the text, including Ptolemy's own explanation of how to re-plot his maps from the data he had collected and collated.

Ptolemy's association of Bath with the Belgae, contrasting with the Late Iron Age coin evidence which points to it being within Dobunnic territory, has led to suggestions that he made a mistake. Given the complications of compiling an atlas of Britain from the distance of Alexandria and making sense of a possibly incomplete set of data from a distant province this is not an unreasonable suggestion. However, Ptolemy's evidence should not be so easily dismissed. Ptolemy states in Book II, Chapter 2 of the *Geography* that: 'Below the Dobunni lie the Belgae and the cities: *Ischalis, Aquae Calidae, Venta*'.[38] *Ischalis* is almost certainly Charterhouse on Mendip (Somerset) and so the overall reference runs from the Mendips (*Ischalis*), through the southern Cotswolds (*Aquae Calidae*), and on to the Winchester region (*Venta*). This suggests a distinct block of territory and the association of *Ischalis* with *Aquae Calidae*, suggests the latter was not just a stray reference, linked in error to the Belgae. This is because both Charterhouse and Bath are relatively close to each other and an association is reasonable; so it seems clear that a place name has not just been dropped into the wrong place in the text. Given the amount of lead used in the Roman baths complex at Bath, there must have been a longstanding relationship between the settlement there and the lead mines in the vicinity of Charterhouse on Mendip. In short, the text makes sense. Indeed, if it was not for the fact that all the other – coin and pottery – evidence insists that Bath was *not* connected to the Winchester region, we would probably just accept it as Ptolemy stated it. However, like it or not, it does seem that for some obscure reason in the second century AD the Bath region had been bolted onto the territory of the Belgae. It looks as if there was a political arrangement that brought this region within Belgic control.

The evidence strongly suggests the lands straddling the 'eastern Avon' were linked by a common authority (which, for a time, looked towards *Venta/* Winchester as the seat of its political power rather than towards *Corinium/* Cirencester). It seems that the south-eastern region of the territory of the Dobunni had been granted to the Belgae in the Roman period. In short, although the 'eastern Avon' valley may have been linked to Dobunnic territory in the Late Iron Age this was 'not a pre-cursor for how the area would be administratively handled by the Romans'.[39] This Roman interference placed Bath and the lead and silver mines of the Mendips within a completely different province of the Roman diocese of Britain, compared with the province it would have been in had it been left under the control of the Dobunni. As a result, it was lifted out of the province of *Britannia Prima* and dropped into the province of *Maxima Caesariensis*. This would have extended the boundary of *Maxima Caesariensis* west beyond the Avon, with the consequence that it would have split the suggested territory for *Britannia Prima* into two; whereas if the Bath region was included in the Dobunnic *civitas* it would unite the two elements again.[40]

If it is difficult to reconstruct the boundaries of the *civitates* of Roman Britain, then it must be admitted that it is equally difficult to identify the boundaries of the different provinces. It is not unusual to read references to 'the Roman province of Britain', but imperial government was rather more complex. By the third century the area under Roman rule in Britain had been sub-divided into two provinces: *Britannia Superior*, with its administrative centre at *Londinium* (London) covered southern England below the Wash and also included Wales; *Britannia Inferior*, administered from *Eburacum* (York), covered Northern Britain up to the fluctuating northern military frontier. By the early fourth century the matter had become even more complex. Four – possibly five – provinces had been created. *Britannia Superior* had been sub-divided into an eastern half governed from *Londinium* and known as *Maxima Caesariensis*; while its western half was governed from *Corinium* (Cirencester) as *Britannia Prima*. *Britannia Inferior* was similarly split. Its southern half became *Flavia Caesariensis*, administered from *Lindum* (Lincoln); while the northern (more militarised) half was run from *Eburacum* and was known as *Britannia Secunda*.[41] In addition, it appears that there was, in the late fourth century, a fifth province – *Valentia* – but its location remains a matter of some controversy, although a location in the north (possibly the north-west) has been suggested. Together these constituted the 'Diocese of the Britains' within the 'Prefecture of the Gauls'.

Just where the Avon valley sat within the political map of the Roman provinces is the key issue here. An overview of the varied interpretations leaves two strikingly different options.[42] In the first option the eastern boundary of *Britannia Prima* lay well to the east of the Avon and (whatever the river's role as a boundary in the Late Iron Age) it lay well within the provincial area of *Britannia Prima* and had no function as a provincial boundary in this period. The second option places the 'eastern Avon' very close to the eastern boundary of *Britannia Prima*. Based on this second option, we can suggest that it may have had some role as a provincial boundary in late fourth-century Roman Britain. However the evidence from Ptolemy suggests, as we have seen, that the maps should be more radically re-drawn, with a loop of *Maxima Caesariensis* sweeping over the 'eastern Avon' and incorporating Bath; thus taking a great chunk out of the south-eastern territory of both *Britannia Prima* and the *civitas* of the Dobunni.

One can only imagine what the tribal elders of the Dobunni thought about this; and, like many imperial meddlers in colonial cultures since, it seems that this imperial fiddling with tribal sensitivities came back to haunt the imperial government, or its successors, at the end of the Roman Empire. By stirring up tribal rivalries the imperial authorities had probably stored up trouble for the future, even if Roman power firmly kept the lid shut on such rumblings in the short term. We might reasonably imagine that the Dobunni had not willingly given up their trans-Avon lands and harboured ambitions focused on regaining these lost territories. This would certainly explain events in the seventh and eighth centuries when the Anglo-Saxon successors to the Dobunni made serious moves on this contested territory. Similarly, the Anglo-Saxon successors to the Belgae made equally energetic moves in the opposite direction.

A controversial but, in our view, persuasive interpretation of Late Roman Britain by Stuart Laycock has suggested that Britain towards the end of the Roman period was beginning to experience a political disintegration reminiscent of the Balkans in the 1990s when a similarly strong governmental control was lifted from a society deeply divided by ancient ethnic tensions and territorial rivalries. Indeed, Laycock argues that the separate nature of the area south of the Avon means it was a likely candidate for the Romans to have removed it from the Dobunni and so contributed to an explosion of resentment at imperial meddling once imperial control disintegrated.[43] This is because it would have made Bath and the Avon a contested area between two Late Roman administrative units. This detachment of Bath (plus land south of the river) from its tribal unit is likely to have injected a note of inter-tribal tension into the area and, as such, may help to explain the later post-Roman kingdom boundaries in the region. The placement of Bath by Ptolemy is particularly interesting if it is taken together with the inclusion of the Mendips as this is very like the area which was later (in the fifth century) carved off by West Wansdyke, and excluded Bath, which the Dobunni seem to have successfully reabsorbed once Roman control lifted. If this is the case then it would explain the transition of the 'western Avon' from an internal boundary of the Dobunni in the pre-Roman period to the kingdom boundary it developed into in the post-Roman era. More of that in Chapter 4.

What is important is that this evidence is consistent with the claim that the 'eastern Avon' lacked a boundary function in the Roman period as in the Late Iron Age. This is a particularly valuable clue, given the otherwise rarity of any evidence for internal political/administrative boundaries in the Roman period. However, in the Late Roman and immediately post-Roman period, the Belgic control of the area (as claimed by Ptolemy) may have been challenged by the Dobunni once Roman authority waned.[44] It has been noted that a number of Romano-British villas along the line of the Avon and in its immediate hinterland show evidence for burning in the late fourth century and this, it has been argued, may indicate inter-communal violence between rival British communities in a sensitive border area, made more sensitive by imperial interference. These villas include, from west to east: Kings Weston (north-west Bristol), Brislington (south-east of Bristol) where four or five bodies were thrown down a well, Keynsham (North Somerset) where a body lay under a collapsed wall, Box (Wiltshire) and Atworth (Wiltshire). Other signs of burning have been noted at villas at Combe Down and Wellow II (south of Bath) and at a group of villas further east at Calne, Bowood, Nuthills and at West Park Field (all Wiltshire).[45]

A whole range of factors may have caused fires at villas, ranging from domestic accidents to barbarian raids in the troubled fourth century and the dating of these fires is far from easy, while a number may have been reoccupied after their fire.[46] The claim they represent a breakdown of order *within* Late Roman Britain has not gone uncontested. Nevertheless, it is an intriguing possibility that they are evidence which testifies to the human cost of the Roman decision to redraw local government boundaries. Even if the postulated frontier of burnt villas does not in reality represent a line of inter-communal conflict, then later West Wansdyke certainly does. This alone should give us cause to pause and wonder just how fractured was Romano-British society in the Avon valley by the early fifth century? Roman interference in the region may have made the 'eastern Avon' troubled waters indeed; and the stress here may well have affected the entire Avon valley as Britain slipped away from imperial control. It is to that sub- and post-Roman period, of the fifth and sixth centuries, that we now turn.

CHAPTER 3

From Imperial Province to 'Failed State': Wars, Boundaries and Disintegration

Roman rule in Britain officially ended in AD 410. From the fifth to the seventh centuries AD, the Avon valley provides evidence for both political disintegration as well as aspects of continuity. To modern eyes what emerged looks very much like a 'failed-state', in which the cohesion that holds a larger political community breaks down and it disintegrates into its component parts. This chapter explores the latest evidence regarding the defensive earthwork of the Wansdyke, alongside patterns in artefact distribution and what these tell us about the communities and kingdoms which emerged in the Avon valley region after the end of Roman rule. Exploring the significance of the conflicts recorded in later documentary sources assists us to identify a surprising continuity in the boundaries of the successor states, both British and Anglo-Saxon. This examination compares the spheres of influence of these emerging kingdoms with those discernible from Roman and Late Iron Age political units in order to both explain the ways by which sub-Roman kingdoms emerged and their relationship to previous arrangements. In this examination the mythical 'King Arthur' and the semi-legendary Vortigern both play a part, as do the early kings of the Anglo-Saxon kingdoms of Wessex and Mercia.

The Avon Valley after the End of Roman Rule

In 410 the Roman Emperor Honorius wrote to the leaders of the British *civitates* (the tribal local government units of imperial Britain) to tell them to look to their own defence. The diocese of Britain was within the Prefecture of Gaul and was affected by wider issues which were wracking the Empire. Those closest to home were barbarian invasions of Gaul, across the Channel, which threatened the security of Britain. This new threat was in addition to security problems within Britain which had been growing throughout the fourth century. Raids by Germanic pirates (Angles, Saxons, Frisians and others) were compounded by Pictish raids from north of Hadrian's Wall and attacks by bands of Scots from Ireland. This is particularly confusing to modern mind-sets since, in the fifth century, there was no such thing as 'Scotland' and this only formed much later as Irish-Scots merged with indigenous Picts to create a new political and cultural unit. What was clear though to Roman provincials was that imperial forces were finding it increasingly difficult to guarantee security. Some of the villas burned along the Avon valley may have suffered destruction at the hands of raiding Scots but this cannot be proved and, as we have seen, they may have fallen victim to internal ethnic/tribal tensions as imperial rule weakened.

As a result of attacks on Gaul, Britain witnessed a number of attempts to create a separate Roman-British state more capable of defending itself than seemed possible under the established imperial arrangement. As a consequence, revolts that occurred in Britain in the early fifth century may have been as much prompted by a desire to keep Roman culture afloat as to accelerate the political ambitions of members of the Roman military in Britain. A rebel emperor named Marcus was elevated in Britain in 406, then swiftly killed by troops in early 407; another, named Gratian, was similarly proclaimed emperor in 407 but was murdered a few months later. Political instability was becoming all too apparent. Then, also in 407, a soldier called Constantine was elevated and may have benefited from sharing a name (but no other connection) with the famous fourth-century Emperor Constantine the Great. Reigning in Britain as Constantine III (which reinforced a fictional connection with earlier Constantines) he took his army to Gaul to resist barbarians who had crossed the river Rhine on the last day of 406. The later sixth-century historian Zosimus (living in the surviving Eastern Roman Empire) described how the British 'took up arms and freed their cities from the Barbarians'.[1] It was probably less a unilateral declaration of independence and more a home-grown attempt to prop up the disintegrating structure of Roman rule in Britain. Whatever it was, the British Emperor who pursued his ambitions on the continent was eventually defeated, then killed in 411. This left something of a power vacuum in Britain. The next piece of evidence suggests that the British authorities may have attempted to return to the legitimate imperial fold but without success, for imperial forces had enough to contend with, facing barbarian incursions into Italy. Zosimus goes on to recount how, in 410, Emperor Honorius wrote to the British cities telling them to look to their own defence.[2] There have been suggestions that Honorius' letter was actually addressed to an area of southern Italy – Bruttium – rather than Britain, but the consensus of opinion is that he was writing to the British and that the *Brittia* in his letter referred to Britain. No doubt he considered this a temporary expedient. However, without knowing it, he had officially signalled the end of Roman rule, although there may have been attempts to re-establish it in the following decade. As late as the sixth century, Byzantine diplomatic gifts appear to have been reaching Britain in what was probably an overly optimistic attempt to win friends and influence elites in those western areas of Britain that had not come under Germanic domination.

By the time of Honorius' letter to Britain, the island had long been affected by rebellious 'British Emperors' removing troops to the continent. Constantine the Great had done so in 306, Magnus Maximus had done so in 383; Constantine III had followed in 407. So, by the 'end of the Empire' in 410 most high quality troops had already been removed from Britain but no-one at the time would have thought this was a permanent arrangement. However, this was indeed what it turned out to be and this left British authorities facing a very real security vacuum. This was a situation exacerbated by intensifying barbarian raids. A continental source – the *Gallic Chronicle*, written in 452 – preserves a tradition that in 409–410 Britain suffered devastating raids by Saxons.

In the north, second-rate frontier troops manned static defences and some would certainly have also occupied coastal defences in the south. Other military units of varying quality may have been found in some significant towns. However, the security vacuum would be filled by a different method and this was the well-established Roman tradition of employing barbarians as imperial forces. This was to go badly wrong as the fifth century progressed, and later British and Anglo-Saxon written sources would reinvent this well-tried process as if it was something new and revolutionary: the disastrous or heroic, (depending on source) employment of barbarians which led to the collapse of Roman Britain and the establishment of the first Anglo-Saxon kingdoms. In addition, there would almost certainly have been a private enterprise version of this policy as local villa-owning elites bought in barbarian 'muscle' to defend their political and economic interests, as they themselves morphed from Classical gentlemen into the warlords of the fifth and sixth centuries. Whilst the eastern British elites bought in Germanic fighters, there is evidence (as we shall shortly see) that the western British rulers, in the Avon valley region, bought in Irish warriors. This particularly seems to have been the case to the north and west of the Avon valley and in this, as in a number of respects, the Avon in the sub-Roman period acted as something of a cultural watershed. Alongside these foreign mercenary troops there were almost certainly native militia units raised by the *civitates* to uphold local security or threaten long-standing British rivals. These too will be examined shortly for they are very relevant to the history of the Avon valley, particularly in the so-called 'sub-Roman' period.

It may help at this point to clarify terms a little. Historians and archaeologists use the term 'sub-Roman' to describe the fifth century society in British-ruled areas which was still recognisably Roman, but in a way that was rapidly becoming more dilute as imperial social, economic and political forms disintegrated and were adapted. The term 'post-Roman' is used for British societies of the sixth and seventh centuries that still regarded themselves as distinct from the Anglo-Saxon settlements further to the east but looked anything but Roman. They themselves, though, clearly thought they were the inheritors and embodiment of *Romanitas* and, despite looking and acting remarkably like the new Germanic warlord kingdoms forming to their east, they considered themselves, in contrast, to be the last bastions of Classical civilisation. This distinction was certainly true in religious terms since Christianity – probably a minority faith in the late fourth century, despite official support by the Late Roman government – had by the sixth century become one of the defining features of the British communities of western Britain. This process had probably been accelerated by a desire to ideologically distance themselves from the pagan society of the Anglo-Saxon kingdoms. Evidence of this has emerged at Bath from the fifth century.

What seems undeniable is that change at the end of Roman Britain was seismic. Most studies of the collapse of complex societies find that the successor society is a reduced-scale, more localised, less specialised and less complex but recognisably related society to that which has gone before. This was not the case in Britain in the fifth century. Here the change was almost absolute. It suggests more than a collapse of social structure and looks like a collapse of identity;[3] as if many within British society had simply given up on the imperial project as its systems imploded and infrastructure collapsed. As one recent study has put it: 'Roman society, economy and culture went into meltdown before 430' and a direct consequence was the undermining of the 'social value' of what had once seemed a permanent and desirable Roman identity.[4] A comparable view of the rapid end of Roman culture has gone further and suggested it was a combination of local rebellions, disease, climatic deterioration as well as *small scale* Germanic invasion which led to the end of Roman Britain.[5] Consequently, Britain effectively rejected Roman government with its high taxes, insecurity, blocked access to high imperial office and brutal repression of rebellion. Britain was too far from the imperial core of the Empire to benefit from membership of that Empire, whilst very vulnerable to changes affecting that centre. The province was – as Late Roman written sources insist – prone to separatist rebellion. This, rather than large-scale Germanic invasion, ended imperial rule. In fact, the logistics of massive Anglo-Saxon folk movement are almost impossible to imagine. In about 410 (following the failure of the campaign on the continent of the 'British Emperor' Constantine III and the expulsion of his government officials from Britain) 'the Britons used their chance not merely to oust the government of a failed usurper, but to break with the empire altogether'.[6] As a result, the end of Roman rule was more complete in Britain than in Gaul or elsewhere in the western Empire. It was only after this that invasions of an Anglo-Saxon elite led to conflict with (and eventual defeat of) independent Britons. We may argue over the extent of Anglo-Saxon settlement – it actually looks to have been a folk movement in East Anglia, but an elite intervention in southern Britain – but the depth of the fall from 'Roman-style' society seems undeniable, even if this may have been a trajectory whose start-date was further back in the fourth century and then accelerated after 400. Overall though, despite these reservations, this fairly persuasive argument suggests that at least a generation separates the end of Roman Britain (*c.* 410) from the Anglo-Saxon conquests (after *c.* 440). However on one bank of the Avon there appears to have been more commitment to keeping the 'imperial project' alive than on the other bank. This reminds us that even if the British rejected imperial government in the fifth century, many were still committed to keeping alive their own local version of 'Roman identity'; picking and choosing the characteristics they still found appealing.

What seems clear is that, despite the almost invisible nature of British society in the fifth and sixth centuries, there was not a catastrophic collapse in population. The traditional interpretation of population collapse, accompanying the social and economic collapse is no longer widely held. This can be seen most clearly in population estimates for Late Roman Britain in modern academic sources: 1.5 million in the 1930s, 2 million by the late 1960s, 3 million in the early 1990s, 4 million by the early twenty-first century. Numbers are up due to the increased discovery of rural settlements. The fall in population, which finally happened, occurred well after the end of the Empire. By 1086 the population may have been in the region of 2.5 million, but this fall was a product of the Anglo-Saxon period. Incidentally, it then rose to perhaps as high as 5.5 million in 1300, collapsed to 2.5 million by 1377 (post Black Death), hit a low, *c.* 1450, of about 2 million and by 1750 stood at about 7 million.[7] In Norfolk, aerial surveys suggest one Late Romano-British settlement per square kilometre. In addition, pollen analysis suggests no population crash in the years 400–600. Despite this, the lack of archaeological evidence for the British population has rendered them almost invisible.

A key point to consider in explaining the 'invisibility' of the British population in the fifth century is that it was an elite, the military, and urban dwellers who actually were so 'visible' before this. Ordinary rural communities were always less 'visible' and it was the collapse of Roman industry and the end of the mass production of goods that suddenly made large numbers of the population apparently 'vanish' in the fifth century. What really occurred was that they ceased using (and the poor had always used less than those higher up the social scale) Roman-style coinage, pottery and building technologies. Furthermore, those who had once communicated their power and wealth through the ostentatious display of such things had to reinvent themselves and their elite status by communicating it in different ways.

Alongside these changes, we should consider that by, the fifth century, the Romano-British were probably culturally disorientated and open to Germanic influence. In addition to this, the mass of the population were subsistence farmers. This kind of society was open to Germanic influence as there was a clear technological and social interface between ordinary British and Anglo-Saxons. This more sustainable culture easily absorbed those abandoning the collapsing Romano-British society. Also, the new Anglo-Saxon elite lifestyle probably looked very attractive and accessible to British people when compared to the collapsed Romano-British one. British elites could employ bodyguards and become the petty warlords and chieftains who came to dominate West Country society, whether it was British or Anglo-Saxon, from the sixth century onwards. Consequently, it is not surprising that the war band dominated society that emerged in the west of Britain looked very much like the Anglo-Saxon society emerging in the east. In this latter area many of the new 'Anglo-Saxons' may have, in reality, been British people who had fallen into line with the new realities of life. This is a process known as 'acculturation'. This same process may help explain the emergence of Anglo-Saxon kingdoms, such as the Hwicce, in the vicinity of the Avon valley which look very similar to the earlier Romano-British arrangements in the region. These 'Anglo-Saxon' kingdoms may not have been as Germanic as they were later claimed to be.

This important fact needs to be borne in mind whenever the terms 'British' and 'Anglo-Saxon' are used. Over time these have become firmly fixed in the popular imagination (and in older academic literature too) as ethnic terms. This view is now often challenged in academic studies and for good reason. Given the complicated politics and turbulence of Late Roman Britain and of the sub-Roman successor states, it is highly likely that these were more like labels (with a strong 'brand-identity') than anything that would show up in DNA. They were 'labels with attitude' rather than products of genetics. This is not to say that there was *no* Germanic migration, nor to claim that there was *no* ethnic tension. Instead, it is a reminder that people with British and Germanic DNA almost certainly mingled and mixed and fought alongside each other (as well as against each other) as *part* of communities that eventually came to carry ethnic labels which can confuse us today. In so doing, they probably faced equally complicated opponents. It would be irritating to add inverted commas to every reference to the 'British' and the 'Anglo-Saxons' but, mentally, we do need to add them when we read these terms.

The Hwicce, referred to earlier, occupied land in Gloucestershire, Worcestershire, western Warwickshire and western Oxfordshire. The kingdom name is still preserved in the place names Whichford (Warwickshire), Whiston

(Northamptonshire) and Wychwood (Oxfordshire). While appearing in Anglo-Saxon records as thoroughly Germanic, their territory was remarkably similar to that of the Dobunni and they were clearly a successor state. The kingdom was almost certainly originally a British one – with centres at the old Roman settlements of Cirencester, Bath and Gloucester – which came under Germanic control and reinvented itself as an 'Anglo-Saxon' entity. By the mid seventh century, Bath (the successor settlement to Roman *Aquae Sulis*) had become a Hwiccian settlement. The Anglo-Saxon names of the rulers of the Hwicce may, alternatively, have been derived from Germanic nobles set over a formerly British kingdom by either the West Saxons or the Mercians. What is clear is that during the eighth century the Hwicce were then absorbed into Greater Mercia during the reign of the powerful Mercian ruler, Offa (757–96). The roots of the Hwicce, though, go back to the emergence of British kingdoms in the fifth century. The existence of many of these sub-Roman British kingdoms (and rulers) lacks literary confirmation but we can recognise their existence in a number of major projects that were carried out in the century following the end of Roman rule. One of these projects has left its mark on the archaeology of Bath.

Recent evidence from Bath suggests that at the temple of Sulis-Minerva (in *Aquae Sulis*) the last Roman re-paving of the inner precinct took place around 300 (termed 'Period 4' in the sequencing of excavated strata in this area). This was then followed by seven sequences of stratified layers (termed by archaeologists 'Periods 5a–5f' and 'Period 6'). Analysis of coins and carbon dating of bones within these sequences suggests that these layers of paving and sediment were laid down in fairly swift succession and that 'Period 6' (the demolition of the temple) occurred *c.* 450–500. The great altar had previously been demolished *c.* 355–60 (in 'Period 5b'). This suggests significant decline before 400 and systematic destruction in the later fifth century. This huge project of dismantling the Roman-era temple coincided with and accompanied West Country refortification of hillforts and was probably a related activity in which British Christian regional rulers mobilised resources to destroy a pagan sanctuary at the same time as building new centres of political authority.[8] It is significant that, when the *Anglo-Saxon Chronicle* records the battle of Dyrham (in 577), it lists Bath as one of the three places having its own British king who was defeated by the West Saxon warlord Ceawlin (the other places being Cirencester and Gloucester). By the time the settlement was recorded in Anglo-Saxon written sources, its Roman name of *Aquae Sulis* had given way to *Hat Bathu* (676), *aet Baðum* (796) and *Bade* (1086); the name being derived from the hot baths there.

Clearly, this pivotal place in the Avon valley had continued to dominate the middle reaches of the Avon and had become the seat of a sub- and post-Roman British mini-kingdom. What is particularly fascinating is that, despite its significance, its influence south of the river (for the ruins of *Aquae Sulis*, of course, lie north of the Avon) was certainly limited. It was a frontier town and would continue to be so until at least the late ninth century. In this it bears a striking resemblance to the Late Iron Age evidence which indicates that, west of the Limpley Stoke Valley, the river Avon had been some kind of cultural boundary within the tribal lands of the Dobunni.

A River Frontier

It is undeniable that, in the fifth century, there were significant cultural differences on either bank of the 'western Avon' and this would support the idea of the re-emergence of the Dobunni and the Durotriges as rival players in what we now call northern Somerset. By studying the pottery it is possible to discern a distinct cultural divide between the areas north and south of the 'western Avon'. Imported late fifth- to sixth-century Mediterranean pottery has been found in Somerset, Devon and Cornwall,[9] but is completely absent from Gloucestershire.[10] This complete absence suggests it is not just a product of limited archaeological discovery but, rather, indicates a political/cultural boundary between the two areas.[11] The largest find of Mediterranean material closest to the Avon valley is from the hillfort of Cadbury-Congresbury (Somerset), which contained not only imported pottery but also glass vessels and gold artefacts. Cadbury-Congresbury is close enough to the Bristol Channel to have received visits from Byzantine sea captains and it may have been from here that this pottery was distributed to the rest of the Durotrigian territory.[12] This imported pottery is not only found south of the Avon valley but also throughout the British territory of Dumnonia (the south-western peninsula extending into Devon and Cornwall). This reveals that the area south of the 'western Avon' was a high level political entity which was involved in the Dumnonian trading network and, presumably, had strong links with the British west. In contrast, the absence of Mediterranean pottery from Gloucestershire means that it would be surprising if the area north of the 'western Avon' was part of this trading network or this cultural sphere. The majority of the Mediterranean pottery is found on coastal sites and so it may be that it was not possible for ships to go up the Severn owing to military control of it further up the estuary.[13] Although this would explain why the elites of Gloucestershire did not trade directly with the Byzantines, the complete absence can only be explained by a major political and cultural boundary. The most common form of sub- and post-Roman pottery in Gloucestershire is organically tempered pottery. The number of find-spots for this type of pottery within Gloucestershire is 'so striking that we may tentatively associate this ware with the historically reconstructable Dobunnic area'.[14] The distribution of these two types of pottery compares well with Late Iron Age coinage distributions, with the pottery being divided along the banks of the river Avon just as the coins of Corio/Catti and Bodvoc were.

The fifth- and sixth-century division of pottery types, outlined above, can also be seen with regard to elite habitation, which again seems to show a cultural division along the line of the 'western Avon'. The post-Roman fifth-century elites to the south of the Avon seem to have based their centres of power on reoccupied hillforts. In contrast, hillforts to the north of the river Avon, despite recently discovered evidence for a limited reoccupation of Crickley Hill (Gloucestershire), [15] were not reoccupied on a comparable scale.[16] To the north of the Avon, eighteen of the fifty-five hillforts have been investigated and although some Roman and post-Roman material has been found this does not seem to correspond to widespread occupation. In contrast, of the twenty-five out of seventy-nine hillforts investigated south of the Avon almost all show evidence of significant Roman or post-Roman activity.[17] The elites in these hillforts south of the Avon were plugged into a far flung trade network. Eastern Mediterranean pottery has been found at 'beach market' site in the South West such as Bantham and Mothecombe, in Devon, and Tregurthy and Gwithian, in Cornwall,[18] while a large number of the West Country sites where this imported Mediterranean pottery has been found in some quantity are 'hilltop fortified elite residences.'[19] Clearly these two patterns are related and the obvious meaning is that these hilltop settlements were the elite beneficiaries of Byzantine trade, or diplomacy, which reinforced their elite status. This frontier nature of the 'western Avon' is a characteristic reinforced by the West Wansdyke. The presence of this military and political frontier confirms the separate political nature and complex relationship between those north and south of the river (see below).

What this Seems to Be Telling us about Different Models of Post-Colonial Society Either Side of the 'Western Avon'

North of the 'western Avon' society appears to have remained more decidedly 'Roman' and there seems to have been a clear pattern of kingdom-formation based on the major towns of the Roman *civitates*.[20] It is significant that the account of the battle of Dyrham (577) associates mini-kingdoms ruled by three kings with the towns of Gloucester, Cirencester and Bath. Assuming that the order in the naming of the kings correlates with the order of the naming of the towns this would make Conmail (or Coinmail) ruler in Gloucester, Condidan ruler in Cirencester and Farinmail ruler in Bath. The kings' names are revealing. Condidan's name was derived from the Roman personal name Candidanus or Constantine; that of Conmail and Farinmail had their second element formed from the British word *maglos* meaning 'king', which clearly projected their perceived status in an act of dynastic propaganda. In the case of Conmail, the meaning was 'Hound King' and was derived from an original 'Cunomaglos', which was the exact reverse of a king's name mentioned by Gildas: Maglocunus. Not that this implies any connection between these two rulers. The use of the British word *cuno* (hound) was common in British personal names, including that of royalty. In the case of Farinmail, the personal name was formed from a curious Latin-Celtic hybrid meaning 'Feast King'. A personal name with the same meaning has been noted in the Gaulish example: Vlidorix. Interestingly, the name Farinmail, as recorded in the *Anglo-Saxon Chronicle*, appears to derive from a much earlier record than the actual late ninth-century compilation of the *Chronicle* itself, since its spelling was not affected by the seventh-century change in Welsh linguistics that would eventually turn this name into Old Welsh 'Fernmail'. This surprising feature, alongside the unusual mixture of Latin and Celtic elements and the lack of other evidence for the transmission of such early material into the later *Chronicle*, has led some experts to suggest that the early spelling of the name was due to a scribal error; and that the original form was not recorded as early as it appears and that the 'Dyrham triad' represents nothing more than a later composite, made up of the names of British rulers killed by Anglo-Saxons and assigned – erroneously – to this battle-entry.[21] This, though, seems too negative an interpretation. The simple reality is that we do not know how old some of the *Chronicle*'s sources were (that is the problem of the *Chronicle*) and the impression of mini-kingdoms ruled by kings bearing well attested 'Roman' and 'royal British' personal names is entirely consistent with other evidence for the kind of successor states that had emerged by the late sixth century north and west of the Avon. These were focused on Roman towns.

This does not mean that these 'towns' continued to have any functions that would impress a Roman town planner. The reality was probably a royal centre within a crumbling ruin or a defended site on the edge of a scene of urban decay. Indeed, at Cirencester, the presence of sub-Roman grass-tempered pottery in the town's amphitheatre area suggests that this – not the ruins of *Corinium* – was what constituted the base of this Cotswolds mini-kingdom in the fifth and sixth centuries. Something similar must have happened at the mini-kingdom of Bath but, as yet, we cannot locate or suggest its sub-Roman royal site. This was a massive come-down from former architectural and organisational complexities. However, for those who fought to preserve the legacy of the Roman past this reduced state was probably enough to be going on with. Times had changed and so had senses of scale; new realities had caused major rethinking of old certainties. It may have been that continuing to use these urban symbols of Roman power provided legitimacy for elites who chose not to move to hillforts but who, instead, chose to attempt to 'sustain the unsustainable'.[22] This was typical of a trend noted by other historians and archaeologists that 'despite the physical degeneration of buildings and infrastructure, society was still organised in a Romanized manner well into the fifth century' and that the intent to remain Roman was strong and sustained the idea that 'the forces of disorder could be kept at bay'.[23] Ironically, this accompanied an almost total and rapid disappearance of all the physical evidence which once defined Roman-ness and so, for example, 'St Patrick's world of deacons and decurions may have been vivid to him, but it is invisible in the surviving physical record'.[24]

The contrasting movement towards hillforts to the south and the continued concentration on towns to the north shows the elites on each side of the river Avon turning to different powerbases and alternative models of what kind of society should succeed the Roman past. All other forms of evidence suggests both considered themselves successors to Roman culture but they chose different strategies for communicating this. Indeed, the evidence of links with the Eastern Roman Empire suggests that, 'The physical manifestations of long-distance contact might be minimal in the fifth and sixth centuries, but the psychological, social and religious connections might have been very much greater than we can now measure'.[25] This is typical of post-colonial societies who forge new identities that, in reality, are actually based on selective use of both indigenous and colonial features.

While the elites to the north opted for continuity with features of Roman rule, those to the south were more consciously looking back to a more ancient and tribal past. South of the river seems to have developed into a society which was capable of trade with the Byzantine Empire *and* adapting hillforts for a modern purpose; both taking inspiration from the distant past and connecting with the present.[26] In contrast, to the north of the Avon the material culture seems to remain stubbornly Roman with a continued concentration on towns and the use of organic tempered pottery which is as likely to be from the fourth century as the fifth or sixth. This distinction is also revealed in the strategy adopted for maintaining security. This brings us to the Irish dimension north of the Avon.

There is a striking correlation in the distribution of a particular type of fourth/fifth-century Class 1 penannular brooch (and enamelled pins), with a cluster north of the Avon in Dobunnic territory (including a richly decorated example from Bath itself) and a corresponding cluster in the northern half of Leinster, Ireland.[27] This concentration of Irish evidence on and to the north of the Avon probably indicates this northern trend of trying to maintain 'Roman culture' was accompanied by the employment of Irish mercenaries. When combined with evidence for Irish settlement in south-western Wales, eastern Cornwall and western Devon it seems this policy was employed in a number of areas within *Britannia Prima*. This is not surprising. For *Britannia Prima* a

Germanic source of mercenaries was not a viable option and the evidence from archaeology seems to suggest the use of Irish mercenaries in this province.[28] It is intriguing that it is only within *Britannia Prima* that the mercenaries appear to have assimilated rather than enforcing their culture upon the territory.[29]

An interesting study (contrasting evidence for sub-Roman authorities in the east employing Germanic mercenaries, while those in the west (*Britannia Prima*) employed Irish in a more controlled settlement, plus British militia) suggests this is the main reason for the great difference in western/eastern Britain after 410 and this strategy in *Britannia Prima* ensured the survival of Roman-style culture well beyond the fifth century and despite the collapse of the most Roman features in the west.[30] Mapping archaeology (e.g. Germanic saucer and cruciform brooches, Irish *ogham*-script memorials and distinctive classes of 'military belt buckles') against the supposed provincial boundaries suggests different provincial answers to defence needs in the fifth century. The contrasting strategies appear to have been: *Maxima Caesariensis* (from London) employing Saxons and Jutes, *Flavia Caesariensis* (from Lincoln) employing Angles, *Britannia Secunda* (from York) employing Angles and Scandinavians, *Britannia Prima* (from Cirencester or Gloucester) employing Irish and British soldiers. Here, Germanics were excluded, home-grown troops were raised and supported by Irish mercenaries, which led to a 'Roman west' facing an increasingly 'Germanic east' and ensuring the longest survival of *Romanitas* (including aspects of urban life at Cirencester and Wroxeter), which, it has been convincingly argued, took much of the fifth century to finally end. This distinct culture survived, even when the former province of *Britannia Prima* fragmented into kingdoms of the South West and Wales in the sixth century. This area benefited from a switch in the pattern of trade (lasting from *c.* 400–550) which meant that the majority of trade with the Mediterranean was conducted via south-western Britain. This is a point we have already noted, although our belief is that this (and the differential hillfort occupation) reveals that, within this broad policy of a Saxon-free western zone, there were differences in political culture north and south of the 'western Avon'. In short, while those either side of the 'western Avon' opted for a similar policy of excluding Germanic mercenaries, this does not mean they were reconciled to each other. Indeed, the evidence suggests these different areas of *Britannia Prima* may have been as antagonistic towards each other as to the Anglo-Saxons settled to the east.

What is clear is that this 250 year transition period, from *Britannia Prima* to the mid- seventh-century Welsh and Anglo-Saxon kingdoms, meant the nature of the eventual Anglo-Saxon defeat of western Britain was much delayed and substantially altered by this western resistance to Germanic conquest. Furthermore the hillfort-based British culture, south of the Avon, would outlast the loss of the more Romanised urban-based north-east of

Britannia Prima in the century after 577. It is significant that mapping the survival of Celtic river names shows the 'western Avon' as the start of a region to the south-west of its course where such names survive in large numbers. In contrast, the 'eastern Avon' flows through an area showing significantly reduced survival of such river names. This clearly reflects contrasting survival rates of Celtic British culture.

The Evidence of the West Wansdyke

What is clear from all this is that there was a dramatic difference north and south of the 'western Avon'. Something of a cultural chasm seems to have run along the Avon valley (at least from Avonmouth to the vicinity of Bath), and this was a division delineated by West Wansdyke.

The West Wansdyke is a discontinuous north-facing bank and ditch which runs parallel and to the south of the river Avon from the hillfort at Maes Knoll near Bristol, via the hillfort at Stantonbury just south of Bath, to the high land overlooking the Limpley Stoke Valley. There is, also, a possibility the West Wansdyke continued north-westwards from Maes Knoll to the hillforts above the southern side of the Avon gorge, west of Bristol. This interpretation argues from a mixture of archaeological evidence and a later minor name, in a deed of 1310, to suggest that West Wansdyke actually ended at the hillfort of Stokeleigh Camp overlooking the Avon Gorge. As a result, the dyke probably monitored all the crossings of the river Avon from Bristol to Bath.[31] The route taken by the dyke generally follows the north-facing slope of the highest ground. This may not achieve the best possible defensive and visible line but allows for a series of strategic high points to be either incorporated into the dyke or sited immediately south of it. This route is not, though, a commanding one and the field of vision is often obscured by the higher ground flanking the Avon.[32] As such, West Wansdyke must be recognised primarily as a frontier rather than as a defensive work, as its route means that it is not appropriately situated to act as the latter. There is no definite date for the construction of West Wansdyke and there are three different theories as to when and why it was built.

The first theory is that it was erected in the early fifth century as a political or military frontier between the *civitates* (soon to become kingdoms) of the Durotriges to the south and the Dobunni to the north. The second is that it was erected by a British community in response to threatened attacks by the West Saxons after the battle of Dyrham in the late sixth century. Finally, the third option is that it was built as a kingdom boundary between the emerging kingdoms of Wessex and Mercia in the seventh century following the Battle of Cirencester (628). Whichever of these theories is correct, the fact that three different scenarios from three different centuries can be suggested demonstrates that the Avon to the west of Bath was a boundary between different groups of peoples for at least three hundred years.

The matter though is still subject to wide ranging debate and it has also been strongly argued that its building was contemporary with East Wansdyke (another earthwork running through northern Wiltshire) and, as such, the scale and the military organisation necessary to implement it negates a fifth century date and suggests these two similarly-named earthworks formed a much later unified frontier arrangement.[33] Indeed, the fluctuating nature of West Saxon/Mercian relations (seeing competition between Wessex and the Hwicce and Mercia from the seventh through to the ninth century) leaves the possibility open that the whole Wansdyke frontier was an unfinished project.[34] However, whether it was a fifth-century boundary between British polities, a sixth century British response to Anglo-Saxon aggression, or a Middle Saxon frontier between Wessex and Mercia its western length at least confirms the 'western Avon' as demarcating a frontier.

Recent exploration tends to suggest it was, in fact, a fifth century construction; although it may have incorporated prehistoric features which points to an earlier boundary following the same approximate line.[35] Having examined the evidence carefully, the conclusion in this study is, firstly, West Wansdyke was *fifth century* in date and, secondly, West and East Wansdyke were *not part* of a united frontier. This is why we refer to them as 'West' and 'East' Wansdyke to differentiate them; both earthworks are actually simply called 'Wansdyke'. Indeed, there is reason to suppose that East Wansdyke may have been constructed at least a century later. This interpretation requires justification.

Firstly, the persuasive view that West Wansdyke is a British construction and either fifth- or sixth-century in date needs a little more explanation. Given how little we know about military organisation in the sub-Roman period, it seems too much to dismiss their ability to erect such a monument out of hand especially if there are two completely different dykes. The anchoring of West Wansdyke on hillforts and the naming of it after the Anglo-Saxon god Woden also casts doubts on a later date. The inclusion of hillforts would fit much better with the refortification of hillforts by emerging British kingdoms in the fifth and sixth centuries.[36] In addition, by calling it 'Woden's ditch', the Anglo-Saxons who named it can be interpreted as attesting to how ancient it was and, as such, its name is more likely to be an invention by tenth-century Anglo-Saxon Christians.[37] This last point though does not indicate when the actual dyke was dug. Recent excavation though may help in this matter. The most recent investigation shows the form of the dyke is regular and the overall dimensions are extremely consistent.[38] These dimensions are also completely consistent with Roman military construction and 'ankle-breaker' style ditches.

It also corresponds closely in its measurements, form and construction details with those given by the Roman military writer, Vegetius, in his work *Epitome of Military Science* (*Epitoma Rei Militaris*).[39] This places Wansdyke solidly within the Roman tradition and therefore most likely within a sub-Roman fifth-century context. In the writing of the sixth-century British churchman, Gildas (*On the Ruin of Britain*) he criticises the construction of earth banks and dykes as defensive features and if West Wansdyke was built in this period, then it may be one of the dykes to which he was referring. He also implies there was a separate military force within his community;[40] and if this was the case then it would refute the idea that the peoples of the sub-Roman period were incapable of the military organisation necessary for the building of such a dyke.

A separate study has suggested the reason for this sub-Roman building project was an attempt by the Durotriges to assert their authority in the previously Dobunni territory that had made up the western part of the *civitas* of the Belgae. At some stage, during such a conflict, the Durotriges could have moved north to occupy the territory coveted by the Dobunni.[41] The Dobunnic territory to the south of the Avon seems to have been distinctly different and it is probably no accident that the Romans chose to include this part into the *civitas* of the Belgae, and it is this territory that seems to have been lost to the Durotriges in the sub-Roman period with the construction of West Wansdyke on its northern border.[42]

Secondly, the interpretation that 'West' and 'East' Wansdyke are separate frontier dykes also needs explanation. This is the interpretation favoured in this study and is based on the very different scale of the two dykes and the lack of categorical evidence for continuation of the East Wansdyke west of Morgan's Hill (Wiltshire). There is also a striking lack of Old English references to Wansdyke in this 'gap'. This is despite the existence of a number of Old English charters for this area of north-west Wiltshire in which one would expect references to Wansdyke to occur. It is noteworthy that there are many references to Wansdyke in charters referring to land either side of this gap. Later references to Wansdyke in this gap seem no more than medieval and even more modern speculation and are no substitute for the silence from the Old English sources. This would explain a reference, in the fifteenth-century copy of *Survey A* of the *Cartulary of Shaftesbury Abbey*, to '*Wadenesdich*', near the otherwise unidentified settlement of *Tortelee*.[43] It was probably prompted by the course of the Roman road leading from Bath to Mildenhall. In both Wraxall and Atworth parishes the northern parish boundaries follow this Roman road. Similarly, the *Perambulation of Melksham Forest*, c. 1300, describes two sections of the Roman road as '*Wodenes Ditch*'.[44] However, the Old English sources offer no evidence for Wansdyke in this area and the Bradford on Avon charter of 1001 describes the line of the road as '*þe kinges imare*' ('the king's boundary') and '*alfgares imare*' ('Alfgar's boundary'). Wansdyke is never mentioned.[45] In short, it is probably best to conclude the frontier represented by the two dykes was either unfinished or always discontinuous, though later sharing a common name. This would then be consistent with the view that Late Iron Age, Roman and post-Roman polities based in Wiltshire considered their north-western spheres of influence extended into the southern Cotswolds, to the west of the 'eastern Avon', until blocked by the annexation of the Hwicce into Mercia during the late seventh century. Even then, this did not force a retreat to the line of the Avon for the frontiers of Wessex, Wiltshire and the diocese of Ramsbury. Even if it could be proved that the two dykes were in fact continuous this would not undermine these conclusions since the 'Wansdyke frontier' proved to be a transient border despite its impressive size and the effort expended on its construction. This was the case whether it was built in response to a fifth-century 'non-event',[46] and was soon rendered redundant by changing strategic circumstances or was a product of the later and better attested rivalry between Wessex and Mercia. In this study though, we conclude that the two dykes were separate projects and built at different times.

If, as argued here, the West Wansdyke (whatever the reasons for its later Anglo-Saxon name) was a British earthwork it is possible to envisage two likely scenarios that gave rise to its construction. The first scenario would be inter-tribal conflict as Roman rule ended. The correspondence between the line of the West Wansdyke and the burnt villas at Kings Weston, Brislington, Keynsham, Combe Down and Wellow II may suggest this. The existence of West Wansdyke built along the northern border of the lost Dobunnic territory, in addition to the cultural differences outlined above, suggests that the Durotriges were ultimately successful in annexing this previously Dobunnic region.[47] The burnt villas therefore may have been located on a frontier that needed defending from northern attack. The mapping of fourth-century belt fittings and buckles has shown a cluster in Wiltshire and one just north of Mildenhall which is further evidence for British military (tribal militia) activity in this area.[48] The evidence of squatter occupation in a number of the villas, such as the cooking platform built in the main corridor of the Keynsham villa, can be argued to be refugee occupation caused by this border conflict.[49] The existence of a post-Roman earthwork combined with concentrations of belt fittings, hoards and villa burnings all points to the possibility of conflict. These two groups of conflicting peoples can be seen in the pre-Roman numismatic records, the fifth-century ceramic records, the line of West Wansdyke and the possible pattern of conflict north of West Wansdyke.[50] As such, the 'western Avon' seems to have been firmly fixed as a frontier during this period. The shift in the tribal territories after the end of Roman rule – probably due to the Durotrigian annexation of that part of Dobunnic territory previously annexed by the Romans to the Belgae – seems to have resulted in the river Avon becoming a disputed frontier between two successor British kingdoms.

The second scenario which explains a British construction of West Wansdyke would have been the loss of the Dobunnic kingdom(s) to the West Saxons after the Battle of Dyrham in 577. This envisages West Wansdyke as a British defensive structure positioned to defend the southern part of *Britannia Prima* from territory which had fallen under the control of the West Saxons.[51] Such a defensive dyke was necessary as the – formerly Belgic – territory lost to the West Saxons in the sixth century formed an entrance into Durotrigian territory and the lack of Anglo-Saxon material south of West Wansdyke shows that it was successful in keeping out Germanic cultural intrusion for a generation.[52]

The Situation on the 'Eastern Avon' in this Period of Disintegration.

With the exception of the examination of East Wansdyke and its relationship (or non-relationship) with West Wansdyke, all the evidence so far has referred to the course of the Avon west of the Limpley Stoke Valley. What of the situation east of there? While the Avon to the west of Bath shows evidence of becoming a boundary between two sub-Roman British kingdoms, the territory to the east of Bath seems to have been straddled by the Dobunni in the period after the end of Roman rule. The evidence pointing this way is controversial and takes the form of military-style belt buckles that may have been the paramilitary kit of sub-Roman militia units. The distribution of Dobunnic-type belts and fittings on either side of the Avon to the east of Bath implies similar cultures on either side of the river.[53] During the later fifth century a 'Severn Estuary Style' replaced this earlier set of material but with a similar distribution pattern. Both appear to be the products of British workshops signalling a new political reality which fused elements of British tribal art with Roman styles. They are more evidence for that British kingdom (or kingdoms) emerging north and west of the Avon referred to earlier in this chapter. But whereas the 'western Avon' constituted its southern border, the 'eastern Avon' did not do so. Corroborative evidence for this comes from a rather surprising quarter. The earlier 'Dobunnic-type' buckles are very similar in style to other metalwork decorated in so-called 'Quoit Brooch Style'. These have been found in Kent, along the southern bank of the lower Thames (with some extension of this distribution north into Essex), and with outliers along the south coast, the Isle of Wight, central Hampshire and the upper Thames. This style was derived from Late Roman official metalwork and appears to have represented an attempt to signal a connection with the imperial era. Its distribution contrasts with a more Germanic set of decorative motifs that appeared in eastern England north of the Thames during the fifth century, which is called 'Saxon Relief Style' and appears to have been communicating a sense of connection with the non-Roman, Germanic, European communities of the North Sea coast. The deployment of Quoit Brooch Style lasted until the 470s, when its use went into sharp decline and it ceases to be relevant to our study. However, what the earlier connection may indicate is that there was a military link between the Dobunni and a Kent-based authority following the end of the Roman period. This strongly suggests that the Avon to the east of Bath may have been connected to the shadowy world of Vortigern, the semi-legendary ruler of Kent in the fifth century. [54] This would seem highly unlikely were it not for a very strange reference to the battle of Bradford on Avon (652) as recounted in the twelfth-century work of William of Malmesbury (see below). The fact that, whatever the dating of East Wansdyke, it does not follow the course of the 'eastern Avon' similarly indicates that the river east of the Limpley Stoke Valley was not a frontier.

Clearly, the 'eastern Avon' did not possess a frontier role and this continued to influence the boundaries of the kingdoms that emerged in the sixth and seventh centuries. As a result, the 'eastern Avon' and land along it was more likely to be absorbed into the emerging and competing kingdoms of Wessex or Mercia, rather than be used as a barrier between them. This situation may have been encouraged by the West Saxons' role as successors to a Romano-British authority based on *Venta*/Winchester. For them the drive beyond the 'eastern Avon' and into the Cotswolds may have been designed to re-impose the authority of *Venta*/Winchester on this region; for it had reverted to Dobunnic control under British authorities based in Bath or Cirencester. As we have seen, British rulers of Bath and Cirencester (and also Gloucester) were killed at the battle of Dyrham in 577 and are described as '*cyninges*' ('kings') in the *Anglo-Saxon Chronicle*.[55] North-western Wiltshire was almost certainly a border region of one of these British kingdoms and Wessex was clearly seizing the territories dependent on these three places.[56] It has recently been suggested that north-western Wiltshire may have been dependent on Old Sarum,[57] but the account of the battle of Dyrham in the *Chronicle* indicates that British-controlled Bath, or Cirencester, are more likely candidates. The whole region seemed set to fall to Wessex and it appears that Chris Wickham's comment that 'the upper Thames was West Saxon before it was Mercian'[58] could be extended to the southern Cotswolds. The traditions later recorded in the ninth-century *Chronicle* reveal that between *c.* 550 and *c.* 650 the West Saxons were highly active in north Wiltshire, north Somerset and southern Gloucestershire.[59] Battles occurred at: *Searoburh* (Old Sarum, Wiltshire) in 552, Barbury (Barbury Castle, Wiltshire) in 556, Dyrham (Gloucestershire) in 577, 'Woden's Barrow' (Adam's Grave near Alton Priors, Wiltshire) in 592,

Cirencester (Gloucestershire) in 628, Bradford on Avon (Wiltshire) in 652 and at *Peonnan* (probably Penselwood, Somerset) in 658.[60] Despite opposition by the Mercians, the West Saxons showed a determination to extend the frontiers of Wessex in this strategic area.[61] The eastern Avon did not constitute a limit to their ambitions.

Arthur and Vortigern in the Avon Valley?

It is with great nervousness that any historian turns to characters as problematic and contentious as Arthur and Vortigern but even they may have had walk-on parts in the story of the Avon valley in this period of its turbulent history. Or perhaps this should be re-phrased as: their literary persona may be connected with events that occurred in the region. This may be a safer way of putting it since current evidence suggests that the Arthur that we now know from Welsh traditions was essentially a creation of the ninth-century propaganda of northern Wales, found in the *History of the Britons* (*Historia Brittonum*) *c.* 828. Vortigern, too, had become transmuted into myth by the same date.

If there ever was a real Arthur we know nothing about him and only the mythical hero remains; greatly overlain with later medieval fictionalisation, most notably Geoffrey of Monmouth's *History of the Kings of Britain* (*Historia Regum Britanniae*), *c.* 1136. From the ninth century onwards, Arthur appeared in Welsh traditions as the heroic leader who had led the fight-back against the Anglo-Saxon invaders and had eventually died in an internal British conflict which had deprived the British of their most successful general. The tradition found in the *History of the Britons* stated that he was not a king but had, instead, acted as a battle-leader and had fought alongside the kings of the British. In this role of heroic warrior he had continued the work of a hero from the previous generation, named Ambrosius Aurelianus. This British leader was one of the few people named in Gildas' account (Gildas makes no mention of Arthur) and was described approvingly as a descendant of those who had 'worn the purple'. This suggests he was related in some way to one of the rebel-emperors of the early fifth century. Like Arthur, he too was successful in leading British resistance to the Anglo-Saxons. Unlike Arthur, there is every likelihood that he was a real person since he appears as an historic character in Gildas and only later had a veneer of myth added by the compiler of the later *History of the Britons*. This stands in contrast to Arthur who was described in mythical terms alongside his more 'historic' achievements in this same source. This suggests Arthur was a myth before he became a man; and the absence of any reference to him prior to *c.* 828, further undermines the credibility of an 'historical Arthur'.

The same could also be said of Vortigern, who also had gained fictional and mythical dimensions by the ninth century, with the proviso that he does at least feature in the well-grounded early eighth-century account written by the Anglo-Saxon churchman, Bede, in his *History of the English Church and People* (*Historia ecclesiastica gentis Anglorum*), written in 731. In this, Bede described how Vortigern had invited the first Anglo-Saxon leaders – Hengest and Horsa – into Kent as mercenaries. Bede seems to have based his account on the sixth-century writings of the British churchman, Gildas, *On the Ruin and Conquest of Britain* (*De Excidio et Conquestu Britanniae*), written *c.* 540. Both then seem to have influenced the account of Vortigern that appears in the annals of the late ninth-century *Anglo-Saxon Chronicle*. Incidentally, Gildas did not actually name Vortigern but, instead, described a person called 'the proud tyrant' who invited Anglo-Saxon mercenaries into Britain and soon came to realise that he could not control them. Gildas did not mention the names Hengest and Horsa either. When Bede recounted this story, he gave 'the proud tyrant' and the Anglo-Saxon leaders names and this was then followed by later writers. It is in fact likely that the leader in question *was* actually called Vortigern, since this name means something like 'High King'. So, both 'proud tyrant' and 'Vortigern' may be titles; or Vortigern may have been his name and 'proud tyrant' a euphemism used by Gildas. However, we may ask, what have either Arthur or Vortigern got to do with the Avon valley?

Arthur's walk-on part in the story of the Avon valley is through the possible location of the battle of Mount Badon. This victory of the British over the invading Anglo-Saxons was first mentioned by Gildas, in a convoluted passage which is not easy to translate. Gildas' Latin can be read in a number of ways so that we are not sure exactly when this battle occurred. However, it was probably fought within a time-window of *c.* 475–500. Gildas described the battle as 'the siege of Mount Badon' (in Latin '*obsessio montis Badonici*') – as did Bede – which has led a number of historians to assume, reasonably enough, that it involved one of the reoccupied hillforts mentioned earlier. However, the account does not say who besieged whom. Similarly, Gildas did not say who was the British leader at this battle. Since he had just been recounting the actions of Ambrosius Aurelianus, it is possible that he thought that he was the British commander at Badon but the text does seem to suggest a passage of time between the campaigns of Ambrosius Aurelianus and the siege of Mount Badon. By the ninth century the battle had become associated with the mythical hero, Arthur. This connection first appears in the *History of the Britons*, written in the north Welsh kingdom of Gwynedd, where the battle was described as the 'battle at Mount Badon' (in Latin '*bellum in monte Badonis*'). It was later picked up by the tenth-century compiler of the *Welsh Annals* (*Annales Cambriae*) who described it as the 'battle of Badon' (in Latin '*bellum Badonis*'). By this time the account had changed from one which claimed that in this battle 960 men fell at the charge of Arthur who carried an image of the Virgin Mary on his shoulders, to Arthur carrying the Cross of the Lord Jesus Christ for three days and three nights.

What is clear is that Badon was a real battle. It may have been fought by Ambrosius Aurelianus or an unnamed British leader. It was later credited to the mysterious Arthur. However, the Arthurian connection does not mean it too must be dismissed as myth along with Arthur; there is simply no reason to do this. The key question is: where was Mount Badon? This is a question that is not easily answered. Some writers have considered that the place name may be connected to the later (and Anglo-Saxon) place name Badbury. Since there are Badburys found in an arc that stretches from Lincolnshire to Dorset, this does not really help in nailing down its location. Anyway, the link between 'Badon' and 'Badbury' is far from certain. What is very intriguing, however, is that an appendix to the *History of the Britons* – called *The Wonders of Britain (de mirabilibus Britanniae)* – describes an amazing natural feature as 'the Baths of Badon (in Latin '*balnea sunt Badonis*')...in the country of the Hwicce'. Since the Hwicce was the name of the Anglo-Saxon kingdom which included Gloucestershire, it is obvious the British writer of the *History of the Britons* was referring to the hot spring at Bath. It seems the compilers of these documents thought that Badon was fought in the Bath area. What is of particular interest in tying down the battle's location is that the *Welsh Annals* list a 'second battle of Badon' (in Latin '*Bellum Badonis secundo*') in what should probably be dated as the 660s.[62] Given the earlier geographical associations, this suggests a British tradition of a major battle in the Bath area in the mid seventh century. Incidentally, we have no idea of the ethnic makeup of the combatants at this second battle of Badon. It would be going too far to suggest that this is the battle of Bradford on Avon (fought in the right area in 652), but clearly, West Saxon war bands were active in the Bath area at this time. In short, the idea that Badon was in the vicinity of Bath fits very well indeed. Geoffrey of Monmouth, in his twelfth-century *History of the Kings of Britain*, clearly thought so and made the Anglo-Saxons besiege Bath; a siege that was contested by Arthur and victory for the British only achieved after the battle location had shifted to 'a neighbouring hill'.[63] Now, Geoffrey of Monmouth was more talented as a writer of medieval historical fiction than history but it is noteworthy that in the early twelfth century he was aware of a tradition that connected Badon with Bath. On its own this would not be persuasive. After all, Geoffrey had the East Coast Anglo-Saxons begin their attack (that culminated in the vicinity of Bath) at Totnes of all places; hardly convincing military geography. Nevertheless, when added to the hints provided by other sources, the link with Bath is intriguing. The connection was taken up in the late twelfth-century Welsh story *The Dream of Rhonabwy (Breuddwyd Rhonabwy)*. This work of literature (mythical in its treatment of events) places Badon near the river Severn and names the leader of the Saxon armies at Badon as Osla *Gyllellfawr* (big-knife); who may have represented a garbled version of the name of the eighth-century Mercian ruler, Offa.[64] Clearly, for the later medieval Welsh, a location near Bath was well rooted in Welsh tradition.

This is indeed fascinating, as it makes the Avon valley the likely spot where British and Anglo-Saxon forces clashed in one of the most famous battles of the early medieval period. Even if we discount Arthur as the leader at this battle and conclude that Gildas' account is too vague to offer Ambrosius Aurelianus as substitute leader, this still leaves Bath as the most likely location of the battle (whoever led the British). Clearly, the Avon valley was a war zone frontier at this crucial period of the late fifth century. Given the evidence of hillfort reoccupation in the vicinity of Bath it is likely that the 'siege' involved one of these hillforts. A likely candidate would be Solsbury Hill overlooking the Avon valley and commanding the route-ways up onto the Cotswolds from Bath. Given the later evidence for a British mini-kingdom based on Bath, the most likely scenario is that a British ruler had refortified this (or another hilltop) and that his position there was contested by an intruding Anglo-Saxon war band. This would be almost exactly duplicated a century later, in 577, at the battle of Dyrham – but with an opposite outcome – when another Anglo-Saxon war band again struck at Bath, but this time was victorious, killing the king of Bath. It should be noted that Dyrham is only a short distance north-west of Solsbury Hill.

An alternative scenario would describe Badon as a conflict between British kingdoms, not between British forces and intruding Germanic war bands. This is because Gildas' Latin can also be read to imply that Badon was separated from the – initially – successful suppression of a Germanic rebellion by a period of forty-three years, in which rival British kingdoms engaged in civil wars. Gildas' rhetoric against those defeated in the battle as being *hostes* (enemies) and *furciferes* (scoundrels) could, therefore, be read as political insults against those British forces that he regarded as illegitimate in some way.[65] This is a matter of some controversy and Bede certainly did not interpret Gildas' account in this way (describing the battle as 'when the Britons made a considerable slaughter of the invaders').[66] Nevertheless, Bede's interpretation is just that, an *interpretation* of Gildas' less than straightforward account, and the possibility must still remain that Badon was a Briton-on-Briton conflict. In which case, it adds another layer of evidence to the claim that sub-Roman Britain fragmented into fractious successor states and that the Avon valley was situated on one of the political fault lines dividing these competing groups.

This brings us to Vortigern. All the early evidence places Vortigern in Kent; but later Welsh sources claim he was an ancestor of the kings of Powys (as revealed by an inscription on the ninth-century Pillar of Eliseg, near Llangollen, Denbighshire). These two regions are at opposite sides of the country and it is likely the later Welsh tradition was invented in order to claim an illustrious ancestor for the kings of Powys and to contest manipulation of the past with the rival kingdom of Gwynedd, in whose competing tradition Vortigern was presented as a villain. None of this, of course, has any bearing on the Avon valley and not much bearing on any historic fifth-century British leader either. So it would remain were it not for a very odd reference in an otherwise well-written and fairly reliable twelfth-century source.

William of Malmesbury wrote his *Deeds of the Kings of the English* (*Gesta regum Anglorum*) in about 1125. The work contains legends and stories current in the twelfth century, plus Malmesbury traditions and a Latin panegyric on the Anglo-Saxon king, Athelstan. As a well-connected West Country writer, William does throw light on a number of West Country themes and, even when his account is debatable, it offers a sober and fairly critical version of events. Consequently, it is very interesting to read how he described the mid seventh century Anglo-Saxon conquest of western Wiltshire and eastern Somerset. With regard to the campaigns of one West Saxon ruler he wrote: 'The British...he [Cenwalh] twice completely crushed, first at a place called *Wirtgeornesburh*, secondly near the hill called *Penne*'.[67] These two battles are likely to correspond to the Anglo-Saxon Chronicle's references to two battles fought at Bradford on Avon (652) and then at *Peonnan* (658). This latter battle is usually identified as referring to Penselwood, on the Somerset/Dorset/Wiltshire border. However, the reference to Bradford on Avon as *Wirtgeornesburh* is particularly interesting. The name *Wirtgeornesburh* means 'Vortigern's fort'. It does not seem likely that Bradford on Avon was ever really called *Wirtgeornesburh*, since there is no other record of the name and it sounds more like twelfth-century antiquarian speculation. This means that either William invented the place name in 1125 or that he had access to an older tradition which thought this was an appropriate way to describe Bradford on Avon. This is intriguing because it indicates that somebody thought that Vortigern was linked to the British resistance to Anglo-Saxon expansion that led to a battle at or near the Avon. There is a hillfort at Bradford on Avon and this is almost certainly the one connected to this tradition. Today, this hillfort – named Budbury – is swamped by housing and survives only as a name and in limited archaeological excavation that has revealed a little of its Iron Age ditch. Whilst nothing sub-Roman has appeared in these excavations, the evidence from elsewhere implies that it may well have been refortified in the century or so after the end of Roman rule. If so, it would have commanded the river crossing of the Avon and the approach to Bath from the south-east. As such, it is not difficult to imagine the situation which led to a clash there in the mid seventh century. Anglo-Saxon forces, pushing north-westward from the direction of Salisbury met resistance at an important river crossing which was located on the border of the British mini-kingdom centred on Bath.

Perhaps more important is the fact that William (unlike the *Anglo-Saxon Chronicle*) actually names Cenwalh's opponents at Bradford/*Wirtgeornesburh* as British. As we have evidence for a British political unit based on the Bath region in 577 it may be that this unit had survived the defeat at Dyrham and the death of their king of Bath, Farinmail. In corroboration, the place name evidence from around the Bradford area supports the idea of a continued British presence there. The reference in *Domesday Book* to Cumberwell, 'the spring of the Welsh', and the survival of Cumberland as a field-name (1842 Tithe Map), 'land of the Welsh', to the south-west of Frankleigh and just north of Bradford suggests that the Old English *Cumbra* place name may have been a local area name. This would imply a recognised British-speaking enclave living in this area, into perhaps the eighth century, and one that remained until then resolutely and recognisably British despite the incursions of the West Saxons. The next battle – at *Peonnan*/ Penselwood – was definitely fought against the British; the *Chronicle* tells us that 'Cenwealh fought against the Britons at *Peonnan*, and put them to flight as far as the [river] Parret'.[68] Consequently, it seems logical to conclude the battle of Bradford can be seen as part of an anti-British expansion and as the step between the battles of Dyrham (577) and *Peonnan*/Penselwood (658).

This leaves us with the puzzle of why the name of Vortigern was linked to this battle. The simple answer is that we do not know and with only one (late) source making this controversial connection we should be wary about jumping to any far reaching conclusions. Suffice it to say that either there was some connection between Vortigern's political authority and the sub-Roman rulers of the Avon valley or, alternatively, William of Malmesbury simply selected a name which was well known to his educated audience in order to expand on the limited data that he had to hand. If the latter, why ever did he then choose to link that personal name to this particular battle and then make no more of it? This suggests that he was, in fact, working with a tradition, independent of his own work, that existed by at least the twelfth century and which considered that Vortigern's name was connected with the hillfort overlooking the river Avon and its attendant battle. We can probably go no further than this. Nevertheless, in tracing the history of the Avon valley from an imperial province to a disintegrating 'failed-state', about to be contested by the post-colonial Anglo-Saxon kingdoms, it is particularly satisfying to have the river linked to one of the most famous names from sub-Roman Britain and also to one of the most famous battles (which later gained Arthurian connections).

In the next phase of the history of the Avon valley, though, we move beyond this semi-mythical world and into a better evidenced period of time. It is a period in which the river Avon became the contested frontier between two of the successor kingdoms of what was becoming Anglo-Saxon England, but still retained features of its *differentiated* frontier role that stretched back to the Late Iron Age.

CHAPTER 4

Wars in the West: a Boundary of Anglo-Saxon Kingdoms

From the seventh century to the ninth century, the interaction of West Saxon and Mercian power-politics dominated the role of the Avon as a frontier, but this remained distinctly different either side of Bath. In this a feature of the river frontier, discernible since the Late Iron Age, continued to influence political developments in the Anglo-Saxon period. By studying the location of battles between these two Anglo-Saxon kingdoms, the granting of charters and the competitive patronage of the monasteries at Bath and Malmesbury it is possible to map the shifting zone of interaction between Wessex and Mercia and to explain the distinct pattern that emerges.

Seventh-Century Conflict: Establishing the Frontiers of Anglo-Saxon Kingdoms

At the end of Chapter 3 we saw how, by the middle years of the seventh century, British power in the Avon valley region was eclipsed by the expansion of Anglo-Saxon kingdoms. From the sixth century onwards the increasing Germanic pressure from both the direction of the Upper Thames valley and the Salisbury region turned the 'eastern Avon' into a war zone contested between Anglo-Saxon Wessex and the Britons of the Bath and Cirencester areas.

An initial reading of the *Anglo-Saxon Chronicle*, though, appears to suggest that the only direction of West Saxon aggression was from the south-east. This seems part of a clear geographical expansion which started on the Solent in the late fifth century, expanded into central Hampshire and Wiltshire and southern Gloucestershire during the sixth century with battles fought, as we saw in Chapter 3, at *Searoburh* (Old Sarum, Wiltshire) in 552, Barbury (Barbury Castle, Wiltshire) in 556, Dyrham (Gloucestershire) in 577, and at 'Woden's Barrow' (Adam's Grave near Alton Priors, Wiltshire) in 592.[1] This expansion had also exploded (briefly) into the southern Midlands with a battle fought in 584 at *Feþanleag*. A twelfth-century document indicates that this was at Stoke Lyne, in north-eastern Oxfordshire. The fact that the *Chronicle* records the death of a West Saxon leader, Cutha, there and preserves the tradition that the surviving warlord, Ceawlin, 'in anger returned to his own land', reveals that things did not turn out well, despite the claim that Ceawlin 'captured many villages and countless spoils'.[2] Corroborative evidence lies in the fact that the record concerning the battle at 'Woden's Barrow' adds that Ceawlin was 'driven out', only to die the next year (593). Clearly, something had gone wrong at *Feþanleag*.

The importance of this to the history of the Avon valley lies in the question of where the Anglo-Saxon pressure really emanated from. For, despite the careful crafting by the ninth-century compilers of the *Chronicle*, it is clear that all was not as they wanted it to appear. This has implications for how we read the history of the 'eastern Avon' in the second half of the sixth century and the first half of the seventh century. Reading between the lines it is clear that the version we now have airbrushes from history a vitally important Anglo-Saxon powerbase on the Upper Thames. This is revealed in the career of Ceawlin. He was named by Bede as the second Anglo-Saxon king to hold *imperium* (overlordship) over the other Anglo-Saxon kingdoms south of the Humber. This was followed by the *Chronicle* in its annal for 829 when it recounted the victory of Egbert of Wessex over the Mercians. This annal named Egbert as the eighth *Bretwalda* and Ceawlin as the second one. This Old English term means 'ruler of Britain' and is found, in this form, in *manuscript A* of the *Chronicle*. Other manuscripts of the *Chronicle* use the form *Brytenwalda* or *Bretenanwealda*, meaning 'wide-ruler' or 'mighty-ruler'. By the time it was used in the ninth century it implied a much wider geographical reach than Ceawlin could possibly have exercised in the late sixth century but, even so, he was clearly a powerful king. All the references to Ceawlin in the *Chronicle* name him as a West Saxon and a direct descendant of Cerdic, who founded the kingdom in the late fifth century. He was, therefore, what in Old English would have been described as a *cerdicing*, a descendant of Cerdic in the West Saxon royal line. However, despite this, there is good reason to conclude that (whatever the *Chronicle* claims) Ceawlin was not from the Hampshire-based polity that lay at the heart of officially promulgated West Saxon 'history'. A swift resumé of his career reveals this:

560: Ceawlin succeeded to the kingdom in Wessex.
568: Ceawlin fought the king of Kent in the company of Cutha (brother of Ceawlin in *manuscript F* of the *Chronicle*).
571: His brother Cuthwulf (according to *manuscript E* of the *Chronicle*) fought the British at an unidentified place called *Biedcanford* and seized control of Limbury, Aylesbury, Bensington and Eynsham.

577: Ceawlin fought the Britons at Dyrham in the company of Cuthwine.

584: Ceawlin fought the Britons at *Feþanleag* and Cutha was killed.

592: A great slaughter occurred at 'Woden's Barrow' and Ceawlin was expelled.

593: Ceawlin perished.

Plotting these locations on the map reveals that Ceawlin never operated south of the Marlborough Downs. Instead, his career makes more sense if he is regarded as a Thames Valley Saxon who sought to expand his hegemony in all direction but died in the attempt to bring the Germanic settlers of Wiltshire/Hampshire (historic core-Wessex) under his control. This is confirmed by the annal for 571 and the battle at *Biedcanford*. The settlements, allegedly captured by Ceawlin's brother, Cuthwulf, following this battle, run along a line starting near Luton and ending near Oxford. These seem difficult to reconcile with a leader whose heartland was allegedly in Hampshire and Wiltshire. Now, this may well have been a tradition that became associated with the career of Ceawlin by a later chronicler. The reference to Cuthwulf being Ceawlin's brother in *manuscript E* of the *Chronicle* may have been an attempt to bolt the traditions together through a spurious family connection; the annal in *manuscript F* for 568 makes the same claim for Cutha. The matter is made more complex because a ninth-century fragment of a king-list suggests Cuthwulf was Ceawlin's son. Yet another king-list suggests that Cuthwulf was son of Cuthwine, who was Ceawlin' son. It is possible that all these family details were fictional, as other annals from this period in the *Chronicle* refer to warriors whose relationship with other protagonists is unknown and open to question, such as the Ceol or Ceolric who allegedly reigned five years after 591 and Cwichelm and Crida who perished alongside Ceawlin in 593. In addition, there are references to a man named Cutha fighting alongside Ceawlin in 568 and 584. This may have been the same as the Cuthwine who fought at Dyrham in 577 or the Cuthwulf who fought at *Biedcanford* in 571. It is difficult to tell as 'Cutha' was a shortened form of both names. This is all very confusing. What is clear though is that, whatever the family relationship (or none), the annals for 571 and 584 are more easily reconciled with an Upper Thames base than one sited further south. In this context, the annal for 577 also makes more sense if viewed as an attack into the southern Cotswolds from a base on the Upper Thames. It looks as if a whole range of disparate fragments of tradition have been welded together by the ninth-century compilers of the *Chronicle*.

Too famous to ignore – but too threatening to the official ninth-century version of events which sought to present Wessex as always being a political unity, to describe accurately – Ceawlin's career was awkwardly shoe-horned into the traditions regarding the origins of Wessex. This is an interpretation reinforced by archaeological evidence for Anglo-Saxons on the Upper Thames from as early as the fifth century. These settlers are uniformly ignored by the *Chronicle* but were definitely there and clearly represent the deployment of Germanic troops in the sub-Roman period. This suggests a dual origin for Wessex: one focus being on the Upper Thames, another focus being in the *Venta*/Winchester area (where there is similar evidence for early Anglo-Saxon settlement). In both cases, these were almost certainly settled as military forces by sub-Roman authorities. The fact that the warrior later accorded the honour of founding the kingdom of Wessex on Southampton Water in the late fifth/early sixth century, Cerdic, actually had a British personal name (Ceretic, that later developed into the Welsh name Caradog) indicates that fifth- and sixth-century politics and military deployments were more complex than later written sources portray. Cerdic's successor, Cynric, also had a British name, derived from Cunorix. To add to this complexity there is a strong possibility that Ceawlin's name was also derived from a British original.[3] It may have been related to the personal name Coline. It is therefore little wonder that in the last chapter we advised that inverted commas should be placed around the terms 'British' and 'Anglo-Saxon'.

There is further evidence to support this interpretation in that Bede (writing in 731) describes the early West Saxon community using an alternative name for itself: the *Gewissae* (perhaps meaning 'the reliable ones'). The first use of this name occurs when Bede recounts the conversion of the West Saxons through the preaching of Bishop Birinus, in 635, who was granted a bishopric – revealingly – at Dorchester on Thames. The second reference (referring to events in the 680s) reveals that, by then, the bishopric had moved to Winchester and Bede describes the local Church leader as 'the Bishop of the *Gewissae*, that is, the West Saxons'.[4] The third reference is to a genocidal campaign against other Anglo-Saxons on the Isle of Wight by Cadwalla, king of Wessex, in 686. The final reference, connected to an event in the early 660s, refers to Agilbert, Bishop of the *Gewissae*, ordaining Wilfrid at Ripon. It is only with the final absorption of the Isle of Wight and southern Hampshire into Wessex that the name *Gewissae* was finally abandoned in favour of 'West Saxon'. The implications are clear: the early heartland of the *Gewissae* was on the Upper Thames; in the sixth century they struck into the southern Cotswolds near Bath but failed to expand their territory south of the Marlborough Downs; during the seventh century this changed, when they annexed Hampshire and the Isle of Wight (and presumably Wiltshire too); as a result of this expansion a new name was coined for the new composite kingdom. This fits very well with the idea of Ceawlin being from the Upper Thames and the eventual kingdom of Wessex being bi-focal in its origins.

This has real implications for the Avon valley region, for it means that its British kingdoms were targeted by two centres of Anglo-Saxon power in the decades either side of 600. One was based in *Venta*/Winchester and the other on the Upper Thames. The former clearly saw itself as inheritor of the geographical reach of the old *civitas* of the Belgae. The latter also challenged the dominance of the Dobunnic kingdoms centred on Cirencester and Bath. Neither Anglo-Saxon power regarded the 'eastern Avon' as a limit to its ambitions. It is likely that the battle fought at Cirencester, in 628, was planned on the Upper Thames in a follow-up to the achievement of 577. The West Saxon king, Cenwealh, who fought at Bradford on Avon, in 652, and at *Peonnan* (probably Penselwood, Somerset) in 658 may have had his powerbase either on the Upper Thames or in the Winchester area; it is difficult to tell from the scant evidence.

The last two battles were almost certainly fought against Britons. The *Chronicle* is silent about the ethnic make-up of the 'enemy' at Bradford and also about its outcome, but William of Malmesbury's twelfth-century account of the battle (though he calls it the battle of *Wirtgeornesburh*) indicates that the enemy were made up of British forces. About that he was emphatic. The British, he explained, were perpetually engaged in resistance to the Anglo-Saxons because they deeply resented the loss of their freedom. It was this that led them to oppose the West Saxon king, Cenwealh, and twice suffer defeat at his hands: at Bradford and *Penne* (his form of the *Chronicle*'s battle at *Peonnan*).[5] As an aside, it is worth noting that this fiercely anti-British king of Wessex had a personal name, the second part of which ironically contained the Old English word *wealh* meaning 'foreigner/stranger' and then 'Welshman'.

Interestingly, as we have noted, the *Chronicle* does not claim the battle at Bradford as a West Saxon victory, so the jury is out on what this battle constituted as part of West Saxon expansion. It is possible that Cenwealh failed to penetrate to the Bath area and was deflected south-westward, hence the campaign into Somerset later that same decade. The *Chronicle* specifically states, though, that at *Peonnan* the defeated opponents were British and that it was a considerable victory for Cenwealh. The defeated British were, it seems, driven as far as the river Parrett in Somerset. It is simply not possible to take this at face value since such a pursuit would have been over a distance of more than thirty miles. What it probably implies is that the victory resulted in the annexation of central and southern Somerset as far as the river Parrett.

In Chapter 3 we concluded that the battle of Bradford on Avon was also against Britons. This seems a reasonable conclusion given a British mini-kingdom at Bath but there is the possibility that by 652 Bath had already come under the dominating influence of the Midland kingdom of the Mercians. There is some support for this view from two directions. One is the *Chronicle*'s silence concerning both opponents and outcome, which may have been due to a reluctance to spoil a narrative of West Saxon victories with the insertion of a victory by a rival Anglo-Saxon kingdom: the Mercians. Another piece of evidence is from a very late source in the form of *Æthelweard's Chronicle*, which was probably written *c.* 978–88. Adding snippets of West Country information to the *Anglo-Saxon Chronicle* (which by then was about a century old) this states that the battle at Bradford, in 652, was part of a 'civil war'. Quite what Æthelweard meant by this is uncertain but it implies a battle between Anglo-Saxon forces rather than against British forces. There may though be another reason why the *Chronicle* is silent on the adversaries of Wessex at the battle and why Æthelweard explicitly identifies them as fellow Anglo-Saxons. This is that within the *Chronicle* and especially within Æthelweard's agenda of presenting the inexorable rise of Wessex to a unified control of England, the presence of British adversaries in such an important area of Wessex as late as the mid-seventh century would have served little purpose; whereas the retelling of Mercian/West Saxon rivalry paved the way for the later absorption of Mercia into Wessex, in Æthelweard's narrative.[6] This leaves open the question of who fought whom at Bradford in 652.

However, another pointer in the direction of the battle being against Mercians comes from the fact that as early as 628, 'West Saxons' (probably *Gewissaen* forces from the Upper Thames) had been defeated at Cirencester by the Mercian king, Penda. That the two named West Saxons involved in this battle, Cynegils and Cwichelm, were forced to come to terms suggests that the battle did not go well for them. So, by 628, the British mini-kingdom of Cirencester seems to have been dominated by the Mercians and the same may have been true of Bath. In which case, by the third decade of the seventh century, the only independent British kingdom left in the region was west of the Limpley Stoke Valley and south of the 'western Avon'. What is certainly clear is that the Britons in Wales and in the North were separated from those of Somerset and the South-West and that the 'western Avon' became a boundary area separating Briton and Anglo-Saxon, with the southern edge of old Dobunni territory now under (either direct or indirect) Anglo-Saxon military and administrative control.[7]

Before leaving this battle we need to examine a little of the career of Penda. This powerful Mercian king ruled Mercia from *c.* 632 until his death in battle in 655. He was the last pagan king of Mercia, although his son, Peada, became a Christian. When Penda faced the West Saxons at Cirencester in 628 he was probably not yet king of Mercia. Instead, this should be viewed as an ambitious action by an up-and-coming nobleman who was keen to make his mark. That he clashed with the West Saxons may indicate that he had an – otherwise unrecorded – connection with the kingdom of the Hwicce who had inherited Dobunnic control at Cirencester and Bath. The victory at Cirencester clearly made Penda the dominant military force in the Cotswolds. By the early 630s Penda had secured the kingship of the Mercians. This kingdom was a patchwork of many, once independent, Anglo-Saxon peoples in the Midlands and became a powerful player among the emerging Anglo-Saxon kingdoms in the seventh century and again in the eighth century. Allied with the Welsh ruler of Gwynedd, Penda defeated the Northumbrians in 633 and then defeated them again in 641; and, in 645, he drove the West Saxon king, Cenwealh, into exile. He also subdued East Anglia and made his son ruler over the mixed groups in the south-east Midlands, known as the Middle Angles. In 655, after putting together a great confederacy of subordinate peoples and allies, Penda was killed by the Northumbrians at the battle of the river *Winwaed*, near Leeds. Penda's importance in the Avon valley story is that it was his victory in 628 that denied the West Saxons the control of the Cotswolds. This ensured that the post-colonial kingdom that had emerged in the old Dobunnic territory (with a base at Bath and at Cirencester) would fall under Mercian and not West Saxon domination. The fate of this successor kingdom – that of the Hwicce – will be examined in due course.

The result of gradual Anglo-Saxon incursions consequently led to a four-way political division centred on the Avon valley, with the kingdom of the Hwicce (dominated by the Mercians) to the north and west of the Avon, the British to the south, the *Gewissae* to the north-east and the West Saxons to the south-east. Of these, the most intriguing was the kingdom of the Hwicce, which can first be identified in the seventh century, roughly a hundred years after the first Anglo-Saxon incursions into the Midlands.

The Seventh Century: a Century of Change

By the mid seventh century, it is clear that the sub-Roman kingdom of the Dobunni had morphed into the kingdom of the Hwicce. Plotting the geography of the probably late seventh-century Anglo-Saxon tribute list called the *Tribal Hidage* suggests that, indeed, the Hwicce were the inheritors of the lands of the Dobunni and it is reasonable that we presume that their territory represented a fossilised form of Dobunnic territory.[8]

Overall, though, recognisable 'Germanic' evidence from the region is thin.[9] The discovery of a spearhead of Swanton's type L. dated 450–550, at Quedgeley, indicates the potential for early Germanic settlement immediately south of Gloucester.[10] To this should be added a late sixth-century grave dug for a warrior through the Orpheus mosaic pavement at Barton Farm, on the outskirts of Cirencester. At the recently excavated Tetbury Road Roman Cemetery, at Cirencester, the latest feature on the site may have been an Anglo-Saxon-style sunken-featured building (a so-called 'SFB') which cut one of the Roman graves on the site. It contained sherds of grass-tempered pottery which appears to date from the fifth to eighth century. With regard to Cirencester generally, the fact that, to-date, all four sites that have contained grass-tempered pottery have been found outside the walls of the Roman town suggests that settlement here was probably around (but not in) the decaying town.[11]

The vicinity of the Avon, though, lacks any substantial Anglo-Saxon cemetery evidence. Those excavated are significantly to the east. A large Anglo-Saxon cemetery has been excavated at Lechlade (Gloucestershire) on the Upper Thames, with others at Blunsdon St Andrew and Lydiard Tregoze (Wiltshire) situated between the Upper Avon and the Upper Thames. Wiltshire burials with weapons were unearthed at Ogbourne St Andrew, north of Marlborough, and a large cemetery was excavated at Black Patch, Pewsey, with another at Collingbourne Ducis. Isolated burials in barrows are recorded from Codford, King Barrow Warminster and at Sherrington (all three in the Wylye valley) and also on Roundway Down. Others have been found at West Overton, south-east of Avebury. A larger cemetery than those indicated by the isolated Wylye valley barrow-burials was located at Kingston Deverill. Other Wiltshire Anglo-Saxon cemeteries are found further to the south-east, in the Salisbury area, and clearly tell us nothing about the penetration of 'Anglo-Saxon' culture further west.

Some Anglo-Saxon influence can also been seen in northern Somerset, in the sixth- or seventh-century Anglo-Saxon gold pendant discovered in 1922 during road widening at Burnett, to the south of Keynsham, in north-eastern Somerset. This was found along with beads and a small quantity of bone. Another site consisted of six or more possibly Germanic-style graves at Saltford beside the river Avon (though only identified as such by a knife), in a small cemetery at Buckland Dinham (also in north-eastern Somerset) and also in the sixth/seventh-century phase of an earlier cemetery at Camerton, south of Bath.[12] A secondary burial in an originally Bronze Age barrow on Charmy Down, overlooking Bath from the north, has been tentatively dated to the early eighth century, but on the basis of very little evidence.[13] The place name Publow (Pubba's burial mound) in north-eastern Somerset may indicate a sixth- or seventh-century high status grave beside the Wansdyke, but may equally have been named from a later landowner. A partially excavated building at Coombe Down, south of Bath, seems to be similar to the sunken-featured buildings associated with Anglo-Saxon settlement further east, as does the evidence from Crickley Hill hillfort in Gloucestershire, to the north.[14] Another SFB has been excavated at Avebury and, during the construction of The Shires shopping centre at Trowbridge in the 1980s, three SFBs were discovered, associated with other structures, along with (probably seventh-century) Anglo-Saxon-style grass-tempered pottery. Similar pottery was earlier found nearby at Westbury, on the site of what had once been a Romano-British settlement. Two more SFBs were discovered recently at Hilperton, near Trowbridge . The latter were beside the river Avon and were discovered in 2005. Overall, though, this type of building, apparently so indicative of 'Anglo-Saxon' settlement in eastern England, is very rare in proximity to the Avon. When one was discovered far to the south-west, at Hinkley Point (in south-western Somerset) in 2012, it was hailed as possibly the first discovered in Somerset.[15] The evidence from South Gloucestershire is equally thin with the most substantial being for the extent of the early medieval settlement at Bitton; a settlement associated with a *minster* church (see below). However, nothing from here appears indicative of an *early* Anglo-Saxon presence.[16]

It therefore appears that there was only a very slight recognisably-Germanic presence in the Avon valley region in the sixth and seventh centuries and, given the apparent Anglo-Saxon nature of the kingdom of the Hwicce, the lack of a Germanic archaeological signature in their kingdom and its environs is significant. Clearly, whatever potency the 'Germanic label' had once had, it was losing its significance by the early seventh century. Perhaps this was because with the increasing success of Anglo-Saxon kingdoms in their conflicts with British rivals, it was no longer necessary to proclaim difference as stridently as before. As the dominant cultural force, more could be taken for granted. The traditional interpretation would have it that there were just fewer Anglo-Saxon settlers penetrating westward and that the Anglo-Saxon conquest of the Avon valley was, in reality, just an elite takeover. This is possible but the current uncertainty of what really constituted an 'Anglo-Saxon' in the sixth and seventh centuries makes modern archaeologists and historians far more cautious in explaining ethnic artefacts as being indicative of population levels of a particular group.

In addition, the seventh century witnessed a shift in how ideology was signalled through funerary practice across the whole of England. The so-called 'Final Phase' cemeteries (as paganism gave way to Christianity in Anglo-Saxon communities and as the first kingdoms appear in the earliest records) were marked by a dramatic change in burials. During the seventh century and early eighth century grave-goods became very uniform across England; and Germanic styles vanished, to be replaced by more Classical styles (pins, chains, Classically-inspired brooches). Nationally there is a marked reduction in numbers of excavated graves containing grave-goods, with only forty-two per cent of graves from this period containing grave-goods. There was also a big decline in differences between 'male' and 'female' burial rites. This falls to twenty-four per cent in Wessex cemeteries, where there was a massive reduction in female 'gender burials' using objects signalling female identity. Also, weapons burials reduced in number and occurred mostly in isolated 'male cemetery sites'. There was also the appearance of male graves at barrow sites in contrast to previous mixed-gender cemeteries. This may reveal a reduced status of females in an emerging society that was more stratified and dominated by a male elite. Also, males themselves may have become more stratified with elite males (with weapons) distancing themselves from the rest of society. Where women are more obvious from artefacts, it is in the row-grave cemeteries (possibly lower status community cemeteries) and wearing a costume less ornate and more standardised across England. Perhaps there was no longer need for a high profile female role due to their reduced status or perhaps the earlier female graves had proclaimed the status of competing families rather than that of influential individual women. Whatever the case, something had changed. Consequently, new types of grave-goods appear across a wider area, but in fewer graves proportionally in any given cemetery. Curiously, as kingdoms emerge and as their names and later histories celebrate their apparent tribal nature (e.g. 'East Angles', 'West Saxons', etc.), the grave-goods do the opposite and there is an end to apparent 'tribal identifiers' (e.g. cruciform and saucer brooches) and instead these are replaced with much more uniform grave-suites.

Why this occurred remains a matter of debate. It may have involved a range of causes: acculturation of the British to a dominant style; the need for a wider cultural character in the phase of kingdom building; kings and elites imitated selected fashions of *Romanitas* since this was the last settled community with wide ranging government to which seventh-century elites aspired; the suppression of conspicuous display among groups who had lost out in the competition for local power; the Church encouraged a sense of unity. Although, sometimes termed 'Final Phase' burials they might be better regarded as the first phase of a new era, in which elites across England encouraged a sense of common Englishness (long before a united England appeared) as an expression of a new kind of 'imperial rule' over the former provinces of the Empire. This rule was increasingly Christian. However, the matter is not clear-cut and the new fashion was not necessarily a sign of Christian conversion as some features of 'Final Phase' fashions are apparent in some later sixth-century graves. It may actually be evidence of local elites trying to present a unified culture in response to changes being brought by Christian conversion (so it may have been a reaction to conversion, rather than an accompaniment to it). What can be said with confidence is that ideology and funeral practice was changing in the seventh century and the lack of Germanic evidence in the Avon region is part of this process. It was not just that fewer Anglo-Saxons made it this far west, since many so-called 'Anglo-Saxons' in the east were probably genetically British. Either way, this trend of reducing Anglo-Saxon identity was almost certainly accelerated by the fact that 'culturally British people' made up the overwhelming majority of the new 'Anglo-Saxon' kingdoms in the West Country whatever the *Anglo-Saxon Chronicle* says about the ethnic origins of Wessex and Mercia and however the Hwicce was presented in later written sources.

The Early History of Bath and the Kingdom of the Hwicce

A grant of land issued from Bath in 769 by Ecgfrith, king of Mercia, shows twelve people in the witness list. Of these, four are from the kingdom of the Hwicce. They are named with their titles as follows: Beornheard, Hwiccian *comes* (nobleman), Ealdred *subregulus* (under-king) of the Hwicce, Uhtred another *subregulus* (under-king) of the Hwicce, Æthelmund *ealdorman* (king's regional representative).[17] This makes it fairly clear that Bath was originally a Hwiccian town, but one that was coming within the orbit of the kings of Mercia. It also shows that in the kingdom of the Hwicce, as in many Anglo-Saxon kingdoms, rule was often shared between more than one person. These multiple kingships might be composed of father and son(s), brothers or even more distant relatives. All, though, were 'throne-worthy', because they were members of the royal *cyn* (family). In such a situation the power might be fairly equitably shared; while in other circumstances there might be an over-king (in Latin, the *rex* proper, or *regulus* – a term sometimes used to describe a petty-king in a small kingdom) and an under-king or sub-king (the *sub-regulus*). In some kingdoms more peripheral parts of the kingdom were specifically designated as the area ruled by a sub-king, often a son. This was the case with regard to Kent, once it had been annexed by Wessex in the early ninth century. In the case of the Hwicce, there is reason to believe that, in the seventh century at least, the area bordering the river Avon was specifically designated as an area ruled by a junior sub-king with responsibility for a sensitive border area.

The Hwicce may originally have been clients of the West Saxons, since the first evidence of Mercian domination of the Hwicce is fairly late in the seventh century and from the reign of Penda's son, Wulfhere (ruled 658–675). This was when the South Saxon king, Æthelwealh – who was baptised at Wulfhere's court – is recorded as having married a Hwiccian princess, Eafe. The *Anglo-Saxon Chronicle* records this baptism as happening in 661. Bede tells us that Eafe was the daughter of a man named Eanfrith and that he was the brother of Eanhere and that both were Christians, as were all their people. The reference to 'their people' is significant as Bede clearly used the phrase to describe a distinct group with their own ruler. Along with the fact that Eafe was thought suitable to marry a king, this suggests that she and her father were royal. Consequently, we can conclude that both Eanhere and Eanfrith were rulers of the Hwicce. As such, they constitute its first recorded royalty. The fact that the Hwicce were already Christian by the 660s is further corroboration that the kingdom was derived from the Christian polity of the earlier Dobunni. As a result of this, they had a Christian heritage that long pre-dated the conversion of the Anglo-Saxon kingdoms which had started in Kent in 597 under Augustine. There is nothing in Bede to indicate when they ruled but the fact that neither are referred to in the sources from the 670s or 680s suggests that their joint-rule was taking place at the time of Eafe's marriage in 661. By this time they were associated with the more powerful Mercians. However, since it was Wulfhere who eclipsed the *Gewissae* in the Upper Thames, it is likely that the *Gewissae* were the original overlords of the Hwicce, but had been displaced in this role by the 660s.[18] Indeed, given Penda's victory at Cirencester in 628, this displacement may have occurred a generation earlier. The rulers of the Hwicce come more fully into the historical record during the next decade.

The foundation charter of Bath Abbey dates to 675 or 676 and records how Osric, the first explicitly named king of the Hwicce, granted land there for the foundation of a nunnery.[19] This is one of the first charters issued by a king of the Hwicce and so is a very valuable piece of evidence.[20] The granting of charters to the Church became a mark of Christian Anglo-Saxon kingship and so adds to the picture of the Hwicce as a new Anglo-Saxon force in the region. However, the situation was probably more complex. It is possible that the charter as it survives today is based upon a genuine charter, but that the location in the original has been replaced with the location of Bath. In other words, the later monastic record-keepers at Bath lacked a charter explaining their origins and so took one of impressive age and doctored it to make it 'their charter'. A further complication is that by the mid eighth century, the monastery at Bath was a male institution and yet the charter refers to a nunnery. It is difficult to imagine that it had been a double-monastery a century earlier.[21] The most recent analysis of the charter has concluded that the text that we now have is probably a later fabrication, although it does seem to have been based on a genuine seventh-century document.[22] It is not clear at what date the charter, as it currently survives, was produced, but it was probably forged at a relatively early date, with the aim of 'proving' that the abbey at Bath was a seventh-century foundation.[23] This said, there is every likelihood that a ruler of the Hwicce did indeed found a monastery at Bath sometime in the final quarter of the seventh century.

Whatever the exact origins of Bath's surviving foundation charter, the Osric who is mentioned in the charter (whatever its authenticity) was a historical figure. When he reigned in the late seventh century, Bath clearly lay on the edge of the Hwiccian kingdom. The famous Anglo-Saxon monk and historian, Bede, mentions Osric, which points to his historical significance,[24] and this king also acted as a witness to a charter issued by Frithuwold, who ruled as sub-king of the mini-kingdom of Surrey. This charter was later confirmed by Wulfhere of Mercia (658–674), who was overlord of Surrey, in 672–4. Osric was also mentioned in Gloucester's foundation charter of 679, as one of a pair of local lords described by the Latin term *ministri*. This term was used to refer to a high ranking noble so, clearly, Osric had become rather downwardly mobile since he was not described as a 'king' (*rex* or *regulus* in Latin). This suggests that the rulers of the Hwicce were being demoted to a role of sub-kingship under the influence of more powerful Mercian kings. This occurred in the reign of King Æthelred of Mercia (ruled 675–704),[25] and would be a process that accelerated in the eighth century, under the powerful overlordship of Offa of Mercia (ruled 757–96).

Around 700, Oshere of the Hwicce described himself as *rex* (king) of the Hwicce. However, looking back from *c.* 740 a later document, from outside his kingdom, described him by the titles *comes* (royal-retainer) and *sub-regulus* (sub-king/under-king) of Æthelred of Mercia. In a charter of 777, Ealdred, one of three brothers who ruled the kingdom together under Offa of Mercia, described himself by the title of *regulus* (petty king). Clearly, the independence of the rulers of the Hwicce had been reduced somewhat since the late seventh century. Ealdred ruled in the company of his brothers Eanberht and Uhtred. In this same charter, King Offa gave his own perspective on their relative powers when he described Ealdred both as *regulus* (petty king) and *dux* (leader) of his own people of the Hwicce. It seems that Offa was reminding Ealdred of the limits to his power. This is a reminder of how the power of the Mercians was bearing down on the kings of the Hwicce.[26] This, though, was power relations from the lofty view of the overlord and in the Bath area (and elsewhere in the kingdom of the Hwicce) the authority of a local ruler (whether he or others called him 'king', 'petty king', 'sub-king', or just 'leader') was probably still highly significant.[27] Even so, it looks as if the Mercian overlord was engaged in a determined policy to remove even these semi-independent rulers and replace them with his own appointees. In the 790s Offa granted land in the Hwiccian kingdom with no mention whatsoever of Hwiccian sub-kings and we hear no more of the royal brothers Eanberht, Uhtred and Ealdred. Clearly, Hwiccian independence was a thing of the past and the king of Mercia was by then the undisputed ruler in Bath and on the north and western side of the Avon valley.

A brief flicker of Hwiccian independence occurred in 802, after the death of Offa (in 796). In that year the *Anglo-Saxon Chronicle* records that the Mercian *ealdorman*, named Æthelmund, rode out of the province of the Hwicce and invaded Wessex. The invaders crossed the border at Kempsford (Gloucestershire) on the Upper Thames and fourteen miles north-east of the Avon at Malmesbury. This act of aggression came to nothing since he was defeated by Weohstan, the *ealdorman* of Wiltshire. Both the *ealdormen* died in what the *Chronicle* describes as a 'great battle' but the victory went to the men of Wiltshire and the Hwiccian levies were expelled. Was this a final act of the Hwiccian royal line and in the vicinity of the upper reaches of the 'eastern Avon' too? It is possible. However, a man named Æthelmund appears in charters of the 790s as a Mercian royal official, so it may have been that this invasion of Wessex was launched by an appointee of the Mercian king, rather than by a member of the royal house of the Hwicce. The death of the West Saxon king, Brihtric in 802, may have prompted Æthelmund to launch an opportunistic plundering raid. The *Chronicle* reports that the invasion occurred on the same day as Brihtric's death.

That an awareness of being a member of, what had once been, the independent kingdom of the Hwicce survived into the middle of the ninth century is revealed in a charter of 855, in which King Burgred of Mercia, whilst at Tamworth (Staffordshire), granted land located at Blockley (Gloucestershire).[28] One of the stipulations in the grant was that the estate was exempt from providing support to the huntsmen of the king and the *ealdorman*, unless they came from the Hwicce. Clearly, as late as this date there still existed a sense of being a member of this community, distinct from the rest of Mercia. By this time though, this was a pale shadow of the political community it had once been.

Control of the Church was another method by which the rulers of Mercia slowly reduced the independence of the Hwicce and also that of potential rivals in the Church hierarchy in the Avon valley. By the middle of the eighth century, Bath Abbey was under the control of the bishop of Worcester, until it passed into the hands of Offa of Mercia. It is likely that the prologue to the Bath monastery foundation charter of 675 was written in order to establish Bath as a Hwiccian establishment, closely associated with the See of Worcester from the time of its foundation.[29] If so, this piece of defensive propaganda failed to prevent the kings of Mercia from taking this important border monastery away from the authority of the bishop of Worcester just as they would deprive the Hwiccian royalty of their independence a decade later. At the Synod of Brentford, in 781, the church of Worcester relinquished its claim to the *minster* (an important local church) at Bath and surrendered it to Offa of Mercia. In return, Worcester gained lands in the heart of the Mercian kingdom and also royal confirmation of its possession of other *minsters* and lands.[30] This action by Offa indicates that the Bath estate was already part of the hereditary property of the previous Mercian king, Æthelbald (ruled 716–757). This makes sense in strategic terms since Bath was located in a sensitive border area, facing West Saxon territory.[31] After this date, Bath Abbey was a royal monastery under the direct authority of the Mercian kings. What the rulers of the Hwicce felt about this can only be imagined. The twelfth-century historian, William of Malmesbury, states that Offa was staying at Bath (implying that a royal estate centre was located there) when, in a dream, he was told to found the monastery at St Albans.[32] Clearly, Bath mattered to Offa and it was important to show his presence there.

The sensitivity of the border settlement at Bath was also revealed in Offa's actions to reduce the influence of Cynewulf, king of Wessex, there. He did this by reversing Cynewulf's earlier grant of land to Bath Abbey north of the river

Avon.[33] This earlier grant by Cynewulf had occurred in 757 and had involved the granting of land to Bath at North Stoke, north of the Avon, which suggests that Cynewulf had been attempting to extend his influence on that side of the river. As well as reducing Cynewulf's authority north of the Avon, Offa's incentive for regaining control of the estate at North Stoke may have included the wish to secure for his own control the Iron Age hillfort at Little Down Camp, a site with 'obvious military potential', overlooking the Avon valley from the Mercian side.[34] Whatever the ostensibly spiritual reasons for this earlier grant by Cynewulf, Offa interpreted it as interference in his back-yard. It is even possible that Cynewulf had deliberately done this in order to test the extent of his own authority. That he took the opportunity provided by the murder of the Mercian king, Æthelbald that year suggests that he was indeed attempting to tilt the balance of power in his own favour.[35] If so, he soon had political realities spelled out to him. In a further step, as if to underline the point being made, Offa acquired land from Cynewulf located to the south of the Avon in West Saxon territory.

All of this shows that power-politics in the Avon valley had come a long way since the early seventh century. By the late eighth century the West Saxons had annexed the lands south of the 'western Avon' and British power, in the shape of the kingdom of Dumnonia, was now pushed far to the south-west, into western Devon and Cornwall. As a consequence, the West Saxons had succeeded the British community that had once built West Wansdyke as its northern border and the Mercians had finally succeeded the Hwicce and the earlier Dobunni as rulers north of the river. For the next two centuries the 'western Avon' would become the frontier between two major Anglo-Saxon kingdoms. Further corroboration of the frontier nature of the settlement at Bath is the fact that Offa's son Ecgfrith chose to meet the West Saxon ruler, Brihtric, there in 796; Bath was clearly an appropriate meeting place as it was located on the Mercia-Wessex border. The description of Bath, in the charter issued at this meeting, as 'the celebrated monastery' emphasised the close connection between it and the Mercian royal dynasty.[36] There were clear parallels between the location at Bath, with its hot springs, and the contemporary construction of a palace at the hot springs of Aachen, by the Franking king, Charlemagne. This suggests that the Mercians were emulating the impressive Carolingian style of imperial grandeur and Bath gave them an ideal opportunity to achieve this.[37] As late as 864, King Burgred of Mercia was granting a charter at Bath which implies a Mercian royal residence in the town.[38] The old Roman town at the pivotal point on the course of the river Avon was once more a site of real importance.

Competition Between Kingdoms ...
More on the Spiritual Dimension.

Given the neutralisation of the British and the establishment of a frontier
between Mercia to the north and Wessex to the south, rivalry was high along the
Avon valley. One of the main areas in which their competition for dominance
can be seen is within the charter evidence from the border monasteries at Bath
and Malmesbury. This has already been touched on, above, with regard to
Bath but the evidence repays more detailed examination. Malmesbury was
technically a West Saxon establishment whose premier seventh-century saint,
Aldhelm, was probably a member of the royal house of Wessex; while Bath,
as we have seen, was founded by the king of the Hwicce and later patronised
by the kings of Mercia. By controlling the monastic house at Bath and a
bridgehead of land to the south of the Avon, Offa was able to dominate the
Avon Valley. Thus far we have considered the strategic role of Bath but now it
is time to turn to examine the monastery at Malmesbury.

The monastery at Malmesbury was founded in the mid seventh century,
possibly by an Irish monk named Maildub, and perhaps when the area was still
British. The first recorded abbot was Aldhelm and he is reported by William
of Malmesbury to have been a member of the West Saxon royal house and
this would support the idea that the monastery was in West Saxon hands.[39]
Malmesbury tradition claims that, despite the advance of Mercia into the
kingdom of Wessex on a number of occasions, the West Saxon king, Caedwalla,
was still able to grant estates on 'both sides of the wood named Kemble'.[40]
Clearly, the West Saxons were not about to give up their ambitions in the
frontier zone of the Upper Avon. The charters also show us that Aldhelm was
successful in securing patronage from both the Mercians and the West Saxons
because he recognised the sensitive nature of his establishment's location. We
are told by William of Malmesbury that Aldhelm applied for special privileges
from Pope Sergius I, with the agreement of both King Ine of Wessex and King
Æthelbald of Mercia, so that his monasteries would not be affected by warfare
between the two.[41] That both Mercia and Wessex regarded Malmesbury as a
place to compete for influence is clear from the patronage that both offered
this strategic monastery. The Mercian *comes* (royal-retainer) Cenfrith[42] and the
kings Æthelred[43] and Berhtwald[44] all made land grants to Malmesbury during
the 680s. At the same time, the West Saxon ruler, Caedwalla, was also making
grants to the abbey,[45] as were Baldred the sub-king of West Saxon-controlled
Somerset[46] and Leuthere the bishop of the West Saxons in 675.[47] Clearly, the
competition for spiritual supremacy at Malmesbury was hotting up.

The contested frontier nature of the Malmesbury area is further revealed in
the fact that the Mercian, Berhtwald – described as *rex,* or *sub-regulus,* in the
charter evidence – was, as nephew of the king of Mercia, clearly charged with

holding a sensitive border area in the 680s. Berhtwald is named as nephew of Æthelred of Mercia by William of Malmesbury. Regarding Berhtwald, William commented: 'He did not have a king's powers, but was a sub-king (*sub-regulus*) ruling part of the kingdom.'[48] This appears to have been part of a wider policy of Æthelred of Mercia designed to secure disputed border areas following the death of his predecessor, Wulfhere.[49] In the same decade, Berhtwald's counterpart on the West Saxon side was Baldred, who granted land near the Avon itself.[50] Witnessing this charter as *rex* (king) and described as *patricius* (noble) by Aldhelm, he was a sub-king of a border area, as was Berhtwald.[51] The connection between these frontier sub-kings and the Avon valley extended westwards too, since Baldred also appears to have held authority in northern Somerset and Berhtwald in southern Gloucestershire.[52]

The competition between Mercia and Wessex over influence at Malmesbury is revealed in what was probably the last charter granted by Æthelbald of Mercia in 757 (he was murdered by members of his bodyguard later that year). In this charter, land at Tockenham (Wiltshire) was granted to Malmesbury; but the grant was also witnessed by Cynewulf of Wessex and both kings clearly took a keen interest in this area of north-western Wiltshire. The tense and competitive nature of the relationship between the two kingdoms is vividly revealed by the fact that, on Æthelbald's death later that same year, Cynewulf reasserted West Saxon control in the upper Thames valley.[53] This West Saxon expansion of control in the upper Thames region would have also had implications for north-western Wiltshire, which also bordered Mercia. Despite Cynewulf's humiliation at Bath, it is clear that the West Saxons hung on to Malmesbury even in the face of a threat as large as that posed by Offa. Between the death of Æthelbald of Mercia in 757 and the end of an independent Mercian monarchy in 879 during the Viking Wars, it is noteworthy that only one grant of land was made to Malmesbury by a Mercian ruler (this was Offa's short-lived successor, Ecgfrith, in 796). All other grants were made by kings of Wessex. This limited involvement of the Mercians with Malmesbury contrasts with the fact that, following the death of Cynewulf of Wessex in 786, Offa actively intervened in other areas of Wessex, including northern Wiltshire, until his own death in 796. This very limited Mercian intervention at Malmesbury was in contrast to Offa's active intervention at Bath. It is clear from this that, despite suggestions to the contrary,[54] the monastery at Malmesbury was not on the 'front line' in the way that the *minster* further down the Avon valley at Bath was. It is reasonable to conclude that this was because the 'front line' in the Malmesbury area lay significantly further to the west.

In contrast to Malmesbury, the limited charter evidence from Bath only shows kings of the Hwicce and Mercians acting with the consent of the Mercian king, making land grants during the 670s and 680s. There are very few surviving charter records from Bath but it is interesting that the only other charter dating from the period of the Mercian supremacy at Bath is actually the charter by Cynewulf of Wessex in 757.[55] In the same year he was also granting land to Malmesbury.[56] Clearly, he was active along this sensitive stretch of his northern frontier in that year of opportunity following the murder of Æthelbald of Mercia. However, at Bath West Saxon authority was far from secure. The earlier charter, as we have seen, was later rescinded by Offa of Mercia. Returning to Malmesbury, the last grant of land by the Mercians to Malmesbury was by Ecgfrith in 796[57] and, after this point, there do not appear to be any grants *by either side* until the reign of Æthelwulf of Wessex in the 830s[58] and there were no more Mercian grants in West Saxon territory. The Mercians were clearly being pushed out of the frame by then as major competitors along the Avon valley.

The charters from these two monasteries therefore show us there was a rivalry for supremacy in northern Wiltshire and northern Somerset between the Mercians and the West Saxons in the seventh and eighth centuries. The fact that the seventh-century Mercian kings felt they were able to grant land to a monastery within a different kingdom (i.e. Malmesbury) gives some indication of how important control of this border region was considered to be. The West Saxons attempted to replicate this cross-border interference at Bath but in the years before the Viking Wars of the mid ninth century were not successful in this strategy. Therefore, the situation at Malmesbury, where kings and sub-kings jostled for pre-eminence in the granting of land, was in contrast to Bath which seems to have been very much under the control of the Mercians until the disintegration of the Mercian kingdom in the late ninth century and the last Mercian charter issued from Bath was not until the reign of Burgred in 864.[59] In that year he was at the Mercian royal residence in Bath but granting land in Oxfordshire. While surviving records of land grants to Bath are few in number anyway, it is noteworthy that no king of Wessex granted land to the abbey there until Athelstan did in 931, with the exception of Cynewulf's – soon to be rescinded – grant in 757. It could of course be argued that kings of Mercia too are notable for their absence in granting land to Bath after the end of the Hwiccian kingdom, but the key point to make is the lack of any real competition at Bath once Offa had seen off Cynewulf's attempt. In contrast, the evidence for Mercian kings residing at Bath reveals that it was still firmly within their orbit, despite the lack of largesse shown towards the monastic community there. Returning to Burgred in 864; this was a period when Burgred was asserting a more independent Mercian line, vis-à-vis Wessex, as revealed by his coinage (after an earlier and more cooperative phase in joint minting of coins). His presence at Bath may reflect this more assertive strategy too, with him laying down a marker of his influence on the very border of Wessex. However, by the time of the compilation of the later *Domesday Book* (1086) things had changed. In the turmoil of the Viking Wars (which we will soon explore) earlier land ownership had been disrupted and had been replaced by new grants made in the tenth century. *Domesday Book* lists fourteen manors as belonging to the Church of St Peter at Bath. Of these fourteen, nine are south of the Avon in historic Wessex and one, Bathford, is on the Avon. This is a clear indication that in the granting of charters in the period after the start of the Viking Wars (as Mercia was eclipsed by Viking aggression and land seizure) it was the West Saxons who eventually gained the upper hand in Bath.

It should also be recognised that this technique of placing and supporting monastic houses along the boundary of the river Avon was not simply restricted to Bath and Malmesbury. There were major *minster* churches for Wessex located at Bedminster (note the place name '*minster*'), Keynsham, Bradford on Avon, Melksham and Malmesbury. For Mercia the contrasting chain on the northern bank included Westbury-on-Trym, St Peter's (located at proto-Bristol), Bitton and Bath. We know that Westbury-on-Trym was granted by Offa to the church at Worcester in 796.[60] The original foundation may have dated from the reign of Offa's predecessor Æthelbald. The fact that Westbury is not explicitly described as a *minster* until a document of 804, in the will of Æthelric,[61] does not undermine this interpretation of it as an earlier component in the chain of Mercian *minsters* along the northern bank of the Avon. In that year it was referred to by the name *Westmynster*, which was clearly a well-established place name by that date, while its earlier association with Offa and Offa's well documented activity in securing his southern border with church estates under his patronage makes it almost certain that it was in that earlier period that a *minster* was first established at Westbury. A recent mapping of the extent of the bishop of Worcester's estate at Westbury, alongside that of the church at Berkeley (Gloucestershire), by the time of *Domesday Book* shows how the river Avon to the west of Bristol formed a distinct southern boundary to these two landholdings.[62] The identification of an Anglo-Saxon *minster* at St Peter's, Bristol, is a rather more tenuous suggestion since there is no evidence regarding this church predating the eleventh century;[63] but the fact that its landholding indicates that it was clearly a *minster* at that date makes it very likely that it too formed part of the Mercian chain of eighth-century *minsters* along the Avon valley. With regard to Bitton, a considerable amount of Anglo-Saxon stonework survives in the modern church, and bears testimony to the high status of the *minster* there.[64]

These *minsters* are evidence for royal interest and the use of religious foundations as a means of stabilising the outlying regions of the two kingdoms. These churches, in a period of history before the establishment of a system of local parishes, provided the spiritual care for a large surrounding area and were the dominant Christian presence in an area. Such *minster* churches and royal estates tended to go hand in hand and the sheer number of significant churches on either bank of the Avon implies that they were being used as spiritual markers to define territory. The church of St Laurence in Bradford on Avon is of particular interest as it came under the auspices of and was founded by Aldhelm, abbot of Malmesbury, yet was situated on the northern bank of the Avon. Bradford on Avon was the site of a Roman villa and recent excavations of the villa have revealed the remains of a possible Late or sub-Roman baptistery. It seems likely that the villa transitioned into an ecclesiastic centre, initially of the British church, and was then absorbed into the Anglo-Saxon ecclesiastical structure of an emerging Wessex by the early eighth century. Under King Ine of Wessex, Aldhelm established key church sites along the frontier zone. Aldhelm was based at Malmesbury but was also in charge of a string of monastic communities at Bradford on Avon, Frome and Sherborne and all but Frome have produced evidence of Late Roman Christianity. This is probably evidence of a dual West Saxon strategy of absorbing British Christian structures and existing monastic communities into the Anglo-Saxon ecclesiastical structure as well as establishing a West Saxon presence in a frontier territory. In the case of Malmesbury and Bradford this was on the river Avon whereas Sherborne was facing the (then) boundary with the British of Dumnonia. A charter from 1001 shows a very large estate attached to Bradford on Avon and straddling the river Avon.[65] This may have included a block of land, bounded by rivers, north of the Avon which was the original Romano-British villa estate and which later became an early ecclesiastical estate. This shows evidence not only of a West Saxon church presence on the Avon but also reveals that West Saxon interests in this area, from the second half of the seventh century, lay beyond the Avon boundary. This was then later followed by the kingdom boundary, county boundary and the diocesan boundary in this part of the Avon's course; all of which ignored the Avon. This is in contrast with their interests to the west of the Limpley Stoke Valley, where the river seems to have been a much more definite boundary and where the kingdom boundary, county boundary and the diocesan boundary later followed the river. An adjustment at Bath, in the tenth century, proved to be an exception to this, but more of this later.

Royal Estates in the Avon Valley.

Archaeology corroborates the royal interest in the sensitive area around Malmesbury as revealed in the location of a major secular site, as well as in ecclesiastic patronage. Within two miles of Malmesbury, a probable royal hall-complex has its closest parallels at sixth- and seventh-century royal sites elsewhere (e.g. Yeavering, in Northumberland, and Cowdrey's Down, in Hampshire). This hall-complex has been identified from crop-marks and excavation near Cowage Farm, Foxley, south-west of Malmesbury. The settlement was on the south bank of the river Avon, where crop-marks of over twenty rectangular timber buildings have been identified and these include a rectangular building measuring thirty-two metres in length and ten metres in width. This large building comprised a central hall measuring twenty metres by ten metres, with annexes or separate buildings at each end. This clearly was a high status building and consistent with an important complex. Two phases of construction were noted from the study of its layout. This building was associated with a range of other structures. Five large buildings, measuring fourteen metres by seven metres, were identified to the west of the hall. These, together with the hall, formed three sides of a rectangular open area. A series of fenced enclosures containing additional buildings, on the same alignment, were recorded to the south. The similarity in alignment indicates that all the buildings formed part of a well organised settlement in which construction was subject to an overall plan. Furthermore, a possible church was identified, comprising a rectangular building with a possible semi-circular annexe or apse. This latter feature suggests an ecclesiastical function and again emphasises the high status nature of the site. This measured eighteen metres by nine metres. It was aligned west-east and situated within a rectangular enclosure thirty-five metres by twenty-seven metres. The orientation is typical of a church building and the rectangular enclosure may have created a sacred space within a busy secular complex. The enclosure ditch was 2.2 metres wide and 0.6 metres deep. Closer to the flood plain of the river Avon was located an earthwork platform. This measured twenty-five metres in length and fifteen metres in width and overlooked the river. Its function is unclear. This high status settlement appears to date to the sixth or seventh century. The settlement has been mapped from aerial photographs by RCHME Aerial Survey.[66] This site probably represents a West Saxon royal presence on the Avon which went out of use in the eighth century as this area came under increasing Mercian pressure. It was probably a victim of the contested frontier zone of the 'eastern Avon'.

Settlements such as the one revealed by archaeology at Cowage Farm appear in the written sources from the period with the Latin description *villa regalis* or *vicus regius* (royal estate). These were sited on land run directly by the king and became the centres of royal administration in an area. They provided a base from which royal officials operated and they were the storage places to which taxes in kind were brought to support the royal household. Early medieval monarchs were always on the move. They literally ate their way around their kingdoms. It was to the *villa regalis* that the renders of bread, cheese, ale, meat and meal were brought and stored. They were the support-bases for the king and his household. Evidence for this survives in sources such as the later *Domesday Book* when it refers to royal estates having to provide sufficient sustenance for so many nights' residence of the king and his household. At Chippenham, further down the course of the river Avon, this was specified as being one night's revenue. While the documentary evidence does not survive to testify to such an arrangement at Cowage Farm, it is just the kind of site which was part of the royal network that was later recorded in *Domesday Book*. It would be reasonable to assume that the large number of buildings at Cowage Farm reflects the need for storage of a wide range of goods. The site's proximity to the Avon would also have assisted in both the collection and movement of such products. Such settlements were also the places from which kings heard appeals and dispensed justice. It was while staying at the *villa regalis* at Wardour (Wiltshire) that King Alfred reviewed and confirmed a legal judgement earlier made by one of his *ealdormen* in a dispute concerning a substantial estate at Fonthill (Hampshire). The intimacy of such face-to-face encounters between a king and the local landed elites is revealed in the aside that he did so while washing his hands in his chamber. Such face-to-face encounters could also have a darker dimension. It was while staying at the *villa regalis* at Pucklechurch (in southern Gloucestershire) that King Edmund (ruled 939–946) of Wessex was murdered by a thief, named Leofa, who had broken into the royal residence.

Although the archaeological evidence for the *villa regalis* at Cowage Farm cannot be replicated at other Avon valley sites, the literary evidence reveals that it was by no means unique. The significance of the Avon is demonstrated by the cluster of royal estates along the southern bank of the river west of Bath, as revealed by *Domesday Book*.[67] A number of others feature in key events as revealed in other documentary evidence. It was at Bath that Offa, Ecgfrith and Burgred of Mercia stayed. This is evidence of a major *villa regalis* located there. Alfred of Wessex was staying at the royal estate at Chippenham in 878 when he was almost captured by the Vikings (more of this in Chapter 5). An important royal council met at Bradford on Avon in 957 (examined in Chapter 6). This suggests the location of yet another *villa regalis*, which was also in association with an important church site. Tenth-century charter evidence indicates that another, also near a major church, was located at Brokenborough (Wiltshire), near Malmesbury (see Chapter 5). That all of these last three were located on the 'eastern Avon' may be coincidental but, on the other hand, it may indicate the particularly sensitive nature of this stretch of the river and the close interest that kings paid to it.

In conclusion, by the mid ninth century, the Mercian/West Saxon border was established on the 'western Avon', even if the Mercians were less active players in the diplomatic game than they had once been. However, the border appears not to have followed the course of the 'eastern Avon'. Corroboratory evidence regarding this last point would emerge in the better documented tenth and eleventh centuries. By the 860s Mercia was in decline. In 825 Egbert of Wessex had heavily defeated a Mercian army at Wroughton (Wiltshire) and, in

829, had conquered Mercia. However, the next year an independent Mercian king – Wiglaf – was once more on the throne and Mercia was again back in the game. However, it was back as a reduced force for when, in 853, King Burgred of Mercia defeated the Welsh it was only because he had succeeded in enlisting the assistance of King Æthelwulf of Wessex. How things might have eventually played out between these two rival kingdoms must remain a matter of conjecture because, in the mid ninth century, the whole balance of power along the Avon valley, as indeed across England, was thrown into confusion by the seismic events of the Viking Wars.

CHAPTER 5

War Zone:
the Avon Valley in the Viking Wars

In the ninth century the Viking Wars again saw the Avon valley as a major conflict zone and this chapter explores the evidence for this within the documentary sources and in new archaeological evidence for the *burhs* (defended towns) of the West Saxon kings, Alfred and his son Edward the Elder and their frontier strategies. In contrast to periods before and after the Viking Wars this evidence suggests a consistent frontier role for the *entire course* of the river itself and the circumstances leading to this are part of one of the most dramatic and famous episodes in English history.

The Viking Wars

The Viking Wars started in 789 when a group of Norwegian Vikings killed the reeve of the king of Wessex at Portland, in Dorset. However, the more famous start date is usually assigned to 793 when a great raid devastated the monastery of Lindisfarne in Northumbria. This was hundreds of miles north of the Avon valley region and even the earlier raid on Portland will have had no implications for the communities either side of the river Avon. However, as the raids escalated the attacks (with their associated upheaval) would come much closer, although it would not be until the 870s that the vicinity of the Avon became a fighting frontier in these drawn out wars. These wars would have huge impacts on English history until the final conquest of England by Cnut of Denmark in 1016 and that event itself had one of its pivotal moments in the vicinity of the Avon, although this must wait until Chapter 6 before it is examined.

As the ninth century progressed, the Viking raids intensified. As they did so, they began to impact on communities much closer to the river Avon. Somerset, for example, felt the pressure of Scandinavian attacks in the 830s. In 836 a large fleet of some thirty-five Viking ships attacked the Somerset coast, where they fought the West Saxon king, Egbert, at Carhampton. This battle ended in a Viking victory. The location of Carhampton was once again the location of a battle in 843. This time the battle was fought between King Æthelwulf of Wessex and the Vikings. Again, as in 836, the Vikings won. These Viking forces were almost certainly operating out of the Irish Sea and probably from bases they had established on the eastern Irish coast. From there they were in a strong position to attack Wales and the West Country. Given the access provided by the Bristol Channel and the estuary of the Severn to the western coasts of England and eventually the western Midlands it is not surprising that Viking fleets began to target this seaway. With the Avon meeting the Severn at Avonmouth, the communities along its course were consequently in a vulnerable position.

Viking fleets based themselves in the Bristol Channel, from where they were well placed to raid the West Country and Wales. The evidence for this Viking use of the Bristol Channel survives in the Norse names for the islands of Steepholm and Flatholm. Steepholm is derived from the Norse for 'steep island'; the name of Flatholm is derived from the Norse *flota-holm*, meaning 'fleet island'. The name of the island of Lundy means, in Norse, 'puffin island'.[1]

In 845, an army under the *ealdormen* (the king's regional representatives) of Somerset and Dorset and Ealhstan, bishop of Sherborne beat a Viking raiding party which had landed at the mouth of the river Parrett, in Somerset. In 871 another bishop of Sherborne would feature in the Viking Wars in a manner that brought the full focus of attention onto the Avon valley. In addition to Viking fleets which were operating down the eastern coast of England, a significant number were now very active in the Bristol Channel and Irish Sea region. This is reinforced by an attack on Devon in 851. This may have been yet another example of Bristol Channel Vikings in action. What is very clear is that there was a growing intensity to the attacks.

In the winter of 851–2 an event of historic importance took place far to the east: a Viking army overwintered on Thanet in Kent. This was the end of seasonal raids; from this year onwards Viking activities occurred throughout the year and eventually turned to settlement. In 866, the period of extended raiding (that had started in 851–2) turned into outright conquest. The Viking army attacked York in the autumn of 867 and the kingdom of Northumbria fell. In 868 the Viking force moved south again, this time to Nottingham with the conquest of the kingdom of Mercia as their objective. However, Burgred, the king of Mercia, called on the West Saxons for help and the Viking attack was fought off. This was the same year (according to Alfred the Great's biographer Bishop Asser) that Alfred married the Mercian noblewoman, Ealhswith. Burgred of Mercia had earlier married Alfred's sister, Æthelswith, in 853. It is interesting to note that the earlier marriage between Burgred and

Æthelswith had occurred at Chippenham, sited on the river Avon. This reveals that Chippenham was a *villa regalis* (a royal estate), since Asser asserts that the marriage took place 'in royal style',[2] and that it was located in a frontier zone since it was a suitable place for the two royals to meet. The status of the settlement as a royal estate is further emphasised by the fact that Alfred later left the estate at Chippenham to his youngest daughter in his will.

In 870, the Vikings took over the Anglo-Saxon kingdom of East Anglia, killing its king, Edmund. In 873 they returned to Northumbria to crush an uprising against the client-king that they had installed there. In 874 they drove the Mercian king, Burgred (Alfred's brother-in-law), from his throne and occupied eastern Mercia. Now only Wessex remained of the old Anglo-Saxon kingdoms. It was now subjected to a punishing number of attacks which finally culminated in one major campaign to capture or kill its king. This epic attempt – with its catastrophic effect on Alfred's authority and then swift turn-around to resounding victory – took place on the Avon.

War Along the Avon...

In 871 a battle occurred well to the east of the Avon valley that, by a strange decision, drew that river frontier into the front line. In that year a Viking army based in Reading fought the West Saxons at *Meretun*; the site is unidentified but was probably in Hampshire. There were a huge number of casualties and once again the Vikings won. Amongst the West Saxon dead was Bishop Heahmund of Sherborne. If we only had the *Anglo-Saxon Chronicle* as our source, this would be the end of the matter. However, we have additional information from the late tenth-century *Æthelweard's Chronicle*. Compiled in the West Country and based on the *Anglo-Saxon Chronicle* (but augmented with additional details, often revealing West Country intelligence) it records, for the year 871, that: 'The barbarians won the blessing of victory. Then fell Bishop Heahmund, killed by the sword, and his body lies buried at Keynsham.'[3] The additional information regarding the burial place of Heahmund – '*in loco Cægineshamme*', in Æthelweard's Latin chronicle – was clearly of importance to local record-keepers and reveals a strong local tradition that escaped the notice of the compilers of the main body of the *Anglo-Saxon Chronicle*. It was highly unusual for the bishops of Sherborne to be buried anywhere other than Sherborne or Glastonbury and his burial site on the north Somerset border was clearly chosen as a kind of spiritual marker on the frontier of Wessex.[4] Given the fact that Mercia was facing increasing pressure, this frontier of Wessex with beleaguered Mercia was clearly very much on the minds of the rulers of Wessex. Given the earlier, eighth-century, history of frontier *minsters* along the Avon, the church at Keynsham probably already had a century of history as a border location that stretched back to the days of Offa of Mercia, with his rival chain of churches on the northern bank of the river (see Chapter 4).

The evidence for the West Saxon *minster* church at which Heahmund was buried is slight but compelling. Excavations on the site of the later Augustinian abbey at Keynsham in the 1970s unearthed the shaft of a probable Saxon cross, built into the foundations of the western wall of the south transept. The face is decorated with interlacing in two panels, the side is decorated with a continuous frond pattern, while the back is plain. Another piece of cross shaft was also recovered from spoil from the site. Overall, ten separate pieces of Anglo-Saxon sculpture are listed from Keynsham, making it the second largest collection of Anglo-Saxon sculpture (after Glastonbury) in Somerset. Two of these are now built into the walls in nearby properties.[5] This suggests that the original *minster* was located within what later became the abbey precinct and not in the vicinity of the later (and surviving) parish church of St John, situated a little to the south.

In 878 the war fell in full fury on the Avon valley itself. But this time the focus was on the 'eastern Avon', rather than on the 'western Avon' where Heahmund had been buried. After being besieged at Wareham, in 877 a Viking army killed their hostages and left Wareham by night. Moving westward, they seized Exeter. At this point, the Vikings' plans hit problems. A storm wrecked their fleet off Swanage, forcing them to reach an agreement with Alfred. Finally, they left Wessex. In the late summer of 877, they returned to Mercia and shared out some of the land there amongst themselves and also with the Anglo-Saxon ruler of a rump-Mercia, named Ceolwulf II. According to *Æthelweard's Chronicle*, with his West Country information, the Vikings over-wintered in Gloucester. From here they were in a strong position to monitor events in Wessex. In midwinter and shortly after Twelfth Night, 5 January, 878, they made their move. Under their leader, Guthrum, they almost captured Alfred himself.

The *Anglo-Saxon Chronicle* records that: 'In this year in midwinter after twelfth night the enemy army came stealthily to Chippenham, and occupied the land of the West Saxons and settled there.'[6] *Æthelweard's Chronicle* adds: 'That very foul people [i.e. the Vikings] broke the agreement made under strong oath with the West Saxons and made their winter quarters in Chippenham.'[7] Æthelweard explicitly states that the Viking force which occupied Chippenham came from Gloucester, where they had set up temporary accommodation for themselves; while the *Chronicle* simply says that they had been in Mercia. Asser, the biographer of Alfred, rather confusingly writes: 'the Viking army left Exeter and went to Chippenham, a royal estate situated in the left-hand [northern] part of Wiltshire, on the eastern bank of the river called *Abon* [Avon] in Welsh.'[8] Despite Asser's assertion, the other evidence indicates that they did not go to Chippenham direct from Exeter. Indeed, it is much more logical that they were watching the border from Gloucester since they had suffered a reversal at Exeter and temporarily left Wessex. It is likely that there was something missing in Asser's own source at this point, which caused him to think that the Vikings moved directly from Exeter to Chippenham.

Intriguingly, none of the sources explicitly say that King Alfred was at Chippenham. However, it is usually assumed that he was and this does seem a reasonable assumption for a number of reasons. Firstly, Chippenham was a key royal estate in a strategic position; no other West Saxon royal centre offered such an ideal location for guarding against Viking movements against Wessex from the direction of Gloucester, which was just twenty-nine miles away. Secondly, Chippenham was clearly closely associated with Alfred, given his sister's marriage there and its place in his will. Thirdly, Asser specifically states that the Vikings went on to spend the winter at Chippenham, which indicates that it was well stocked with provisions, as it would have needed to have been had Alfred selected it as his base of operations that winter. Fourthly, the account of Alfred's guerrilla war that followed the seizure of Chippenham, as recounted in the *Chronicle*, reads as a direct consequence of that earlier event. This is all the more plausible if Alfred did indeed narrowly escape capture at Chippenham. Chippenham must have formed the centre of the royal estate which later included Melksham and the Royal Forest of Chippenham. The nearby place names of Kington St Michael and Kington Langley (both north of Chippenham) substantiate the royal interest in the area, as both were *cyninges-tuns* (royal manors), as revealed in the place name 'Kington'. This means that, as such, Chippenham was likely to have become a *burh*, before the great expansion of the system of defended places later on in Alfred's reign. It is significant that, in its annal for 878, the *Chronicle* describes it using the Old English word *geweorc* (stronghold). Sited on a spur of land, surrounded on three sides by the course of the river Avon, and associated marshland, it was ideally suited for defence. The original royal palace was probably located adjacent to the parish (*minster*) church of St Andrew and the market place. The defences of this royal hall were probably reflected in the 'ditch of *Imburi*' mentioned in a thirteenth-century document of nearby Stanley Abbey. This may have been derived from an original Old English form meaning 'around the *burh*'.[9] It was not, though, one of those places later described in the West Saxon document the *Burghal Hidage* (see below) because Chippenham was a defended royal settlement (a 'Kingsbury', of the type known at Wilton and Calne) rather than one of the small towns and communal refuge points later fortified or refortified under kings Alfred and Edward the Elder, and Æthelred and Æthelflæd (the Lord and Lady of the Mercians) in a later stage of the Viking Wars.

Following the defeat at Chippenham the Viking army overran Wessex. Alfred was forced into the marshes of central Somerset, from where he conducted a guerrilla war against his Scandinavian enemies and against those West Saxons who had accepted their rule. After building a fortified base at Athelney (Somerset), he finally rallied his followers around the time of Whit Sunday, 878. From a meeting at Egbert's Stone, near Bruton, the combined group moved to Iley Oak, near Warminster. The next day they fell on the Viking army camped at Edington.

The exact disposition of the two rival armies is unknown. It may have been that Guthrum and his Viking army was encamped within Bratton Camp overlooking the steep scarp of the western edge of Salisbury Plain. Quite what their strategy was in being here is unclear. They may have constituted a large foraging party or may have been deployed to block the movement of Alfred north into the eastern valley of the Avon. It seems clear that their main base remained at Chippenham since *Æthelweard's Chronicle* describes how: 'King Alfred after Easter of that year joined the battle at Edington against the army stationed at Chippenham.'[10] Here, to quote Asser, the West Saxons fought 'fiercely with a compact shield-wall against the entire Viking army.'[11] After a bitter fight the Vikings were defeated. Once again Chippenham played a key role in the proceedings. Alfred pursued the fleeing Scandinavians the fifteen miles from Edington to Chippenham. He killed all he found outside the defences of the royal estate there and besieged those who had retreated inside the defences for fourteen days. By this time they must have been running perilously short of supplies and could expect no relieving force to rescue them from their deadly predicament. Finally, the Vikings came to terms. They promised to leave Wessex and Guthrum promised to accept Christian baptism. The Vikings gave hostages but Alfred gave none; revealing how strong was Alfred's position in comparison with his defeated enemies. The episode reveals the substantial nature of the defences at Chippenham, since they could clearly withstand a siege for some time. This also suggests that when the Viking had earlier captured it, in January, they had caught its defenders by surprise.

Guthrum left Chippenham and moved his army to Cirencester. The *Chronicle* then records the arrival of a fresh Viking fleet on the Thames at Fulham in 879. Surprisingly, given earlier difficulties in holding Vikings to agreements, this did not prompt a renewed attack on Wessex. This is all the more astonishing since Asser tells us that the new arrivals joined Guthrum; which would have strengthened his position. However, instead of reneging on his agreement with Alfred, Guthrum returned to East Anglia in 880 and shared out the land there with his followers. Taking the kingship of East Anglia for himself he changed his name to Athelstan and ruled as Athelstan II (there having been an earlier Anglo-Saxon East Anglian king with the same same). All in all it was a remarkable turnabout of events and the key parts of it had occurred in, or in the vicinity of, the Avon valley.

Fortifications along the River Avon.

Chippenham was not the only defended settlement along the river Avon. After Alfred's reconquest of Wessex he built or extended a network of defended places of communal refuge (unlike the exclusively royal nature of Chippenham). This system of communal refuge places was later extended by his son Edward the Elder and his daughter, Æthelflæd, and her Mercian husband, Æthelred. These defended places are described in a document known as the *Burghal Hidage*, of *c.* 919. The *Burghal Hidage* lists fortified places in southern England, omitting Kent, London and most of Mercia. In the list each *burh* was allocated a number of hides (an area of land, of notionally 120 acres) from which resources were to be provided – both human and material – to construct, maintain and defend the walls of each *burh*.

This document reveals that Bath was one of these fortified sites, with the old Roman Walls ironically being used as fortifications for the Anglo-Saxons to defend themselves against raiders.[12] This defensive use of Bath made it into a town rather than simply a monastic site. We will shortly return to this matter of the defences at Bath. The road system which existed in the tenth century suggests that Bath was already a town in the ninth century – or at least a market centre – before being refortified. This road system clearly benefitted from the pre-existing Roman major road, the *Fosse Way*, which crossed the Avon at Bath. This major road ran from Exeter to Lincoln.

A number of charters refer to the road network heading towards the crossing of the Avon at Bath. While these all date from the tenth century, they clearly reflect a well-established communications network. A number of these charters specifically state that these roads were *herepaths* (army roads/major roads). A charter of 961, in the reign of King Edgar, regarding an estate in the vicinity of the Cam Brook, south of Bath, has a boundary formed by the '*Baeth Herpoth*' (Bath army-road).[13] Another, of 963, also refers to the '*Baeth Herpath*', in another part of its route near Stanton Prior (Somerset),[14] as does another, of 965, also near Stanton Prior. This latter charter is particularly interesting since it provides direct evidence relating to both the antiquity and sophistication of these route-ways. As well as referring to the '*Baethe Herepath*', it also records the '*Ealdan Stanbricge*' (old stone-bridge) and the '*Ealdan Herepath*' (old army-road) as boundary features of this particular estate.[15] An earlier charter of 931, from the reign of Athelstan, for an estate at Priston (Somerset), contains a reference to a '*herepath*' which was also described as the '*Straet*'. This was a term often reserved for a paved road (often based on a Roman original).[16] As if to confirm this method of construction, a charter of 936 specifically describes one section of road, at Marksbury (Somerset), as the '*Stan Wei*' (stone way).[17]

The threat by the Vikings to Wessex also led to the choice of Malmesbury as one of the links in Alfred's chain of defended centres in Wessex.[18] In the case of Malmesbury this clearly built on the foundations (literally) of a pre-existing fortified site at this point in the course of the river Avon. At Malmesbury an earlier Iron Age hillfort (now buried beneath the later urban development of the town) was sited in a highly defensible position, with steep slopes on all sides except for the approach from the north-west. A fourteenth-century document, the *Eulogium Historiarum* – which contains earlier traditions concerning the origins of Malmesbury Abbey – states that the abbey was founded in the seventh century by an Irish monk, named Maeldubh, on the site of a largely deserted but fortified site called by the British name of *Caer Bladon*.[19] The former information is well known from Bede; the latter only from this document. As it comes from such a late source it might be dismissed, were it not for archaeological evidence which corroborates the claim that Malmesbury was indeed the site of an Iron Age hillfort. It looks, therefore, that the point at which the Sherston and Tetbury Avons joined was dominated by a pre-Roman tribal centre. This may well have been refortified after the end of Roman rule but, as in the case of Bradford on Avon, there is no archaeological evidence to confirm this. What is clear, though, is that it was considered an appropriate site within which to place a seventh-century monastery and which, in the late ninth century, was considered suitably defensible to become one of Alfred's strategically placed defended *burhs*. Both the foundation of the monastery and the later *burghal* status were almost certainly also prompted by the presence of a royal centre (a *villa regalis* of the type described in Chapter 4) close by. This was at Brokenborough. The *Eulogium Historiarum* also named this nearby settlement with a British name – *Caer Dur* – and described it as a royal residence.[20] Whether the name (as with that of *Caer Bladon*) was a genuine survival or a fourteenth-century invention, it is clear that Brokenborough was indeed a royal centre. A charter of 956,[21] in which King Eadwig granted land to Malmesbury Abbey, reveals that a huge estate of 100 *hides* was centred on Brokenborough. As in the case of Bath and, to a lesser extent, that of Chippenham, a longstanding royal connection with a place led to its achieving a leading role as a Church centre and as a defended centre of royal government. This juxtaposition of an Iron Age hillfort (possible refurbished in the post-Roman period) and a high status royal centre can also be seen at Bath and Bradford on Avon (where the seventh-century West Saxon saintly royal, Aldhelm, was active). However, Bradford on Avon (like Chippenham) was not part of the strategic *burghal* communal-refuge network, even though both were important *minster* sites and Chippenham was a favoured royal residence. In short, Bath and Malmesbury are the only two named defended settlements in the Avon valley found in the *Burghal Hidage*; although there is persuasive evidence to indicate that they were not alone as defended sites on this strategic stretch of the West Saxon frontier.

Although not a recorded *burh*, recent archaeological evidence from Bristol seems to suggest that Bristol was also defended by the late tenth century and may have come to form part of this chain of riverine defended places. Recent work on the Old Courage Brewery Site – a site also called Finzels Reach – revealed a massive feature; a drainage ditch, or part of a planned urban development south of the river Avon but probably best understood as a defensive feature. If this is so, then it may have been a defended bridgehead for an earlier and differently aligned version of Bristol Bridge, similar to the function performed by Southwark for London Bridge. This ditch lay in an area known in the later Middle Ages as Arthur's Fee and Stakepenny and which came to function as the boundary between areas known as Temple Fee and Redcliffe Fee. By the fourteenth century it was known as the Law Ditch. The suggestion that a southern (defended) quarter existed for Bristol predates the recent excavations;[22] but appears likely in the light of the recent discoveries. The ditch in question had been recut on a number of occasions but the original ditch – identified as 'Ditch 7496' – was clearly a Late Anglo-Saxon feature.

The original ditch was well silted up at the time of a recut when the ditch was enlarged to 12.6 m. wide. It was material from the silting of this recut ditch that provided calibrated radio carbon dating of 1021–1155 and 991–1152.[23] This was corroborated by sherds of a variant of a type of pottery known as 'Bath A Ware' which suggested a date of the late tenth/early eleventh century for its inclusion in the ditch fill. This type of pottery is usually associated with the period after 1100 in Bristol but is also found in Bristol and Dublin in contexts dating from the tenth century.

The conclusion drawn from the overall evidence is that 'Ditch 7496' looks like a 'substantial defensive feature dug in a largely unoccupied area of salt marsh.'[24] In fact, convincing occupation of the site only seems to have occurred in the early twelfth century but the ditch predated this. In its first phase the ditch was a minimum of 7 m wide and 2.5 m deep. In its first recut this was extended to 12-15 m wide. This was again recut as a narrower channel (*c*. 5 m wide), with wattle revetment, in the Early Anglo-Norman period, *c*. 1100–1150. 'Ditch 7496' almost certainly dates from the early eleventh century and the original cut may well be earlier. In its Anglo-Saxon phases it was probably originally connected to the river Avon itself. The dating is consistent with other, albeit slight, Anglo-Saxon evidence from the city, such as the late tenth- or early eleventh-century industrial area found within the boundary of the later medieval city, north of the river, at Tower Lane.[25]

Saying more about Anglo-Saxon Bristol, though, is problematic due to the striking lack of documentation. *Domesday Book* barely mentions Bristol. In common with Winchester there is no *Domesday Book* entry for the town and references to it have to be picked up from other evidence. There is not a single Anglo-Saxon charter for the town. We only know that it existed from a few passing references in the *Anglo-Saxon Chronicle* but even this is so thin that it merely proves that Bristol was in existence in 1051 and of some significance. In this year the family of Earl Godwin of Wessex were exiled and it was from Bristol that his sons Harold (later in 1066 to be King Harold II Godwinson), Leofwine and Swein sailed for Ireland, on a ship that Swein owned and which obviously used Bristol as its home port. Harold Godwinson again sailed from Bristol in 1063 but this time as part of his campaign against the Welsh; and in 1067 the sons of Harold Godwinson attempted to storm Bristol in a campaign that followed the death of their father, in the previous year, at Hastings (see Chapter 6 for more on these eleventh-century connections between the Godwins and the port on the Avon). The earliest dateable evidence in writing that testifies to the existence of Bristol is from inscriptions on coins. A coin of Æthelred II was issued from Bristol, an event which probably occurred in either 1009 or 1010.[26] Coins were also minted at Bristol in the reign of Cnut (1016–1035), probably between 1017 and 1023.[27] These prove that it was a market town since, from the tenth century, coins could only be issued in settlements of this status.

Although the Finzels Reach site suggests Bristol was a significant settlement, the general archaeological evidence for Bristol's Anglo-Saxon origins is thin. This is not helped by the loss of vital stratigraphy on the highest points of what was the medieval city as a result of intensive occupation. There is some debate over the original Anglo-Saxon focus of the settlement at Bristol. It has long been assumed that the Anglo-Saxon and Norman town was centred on High Street, Wine Street, Broad Street and Corn Street within the later walled town. However, the presence of Anglo-Saxon artefacts on the Castle Park site (the location of the later Norman castle) has led some to argue that this was in fact the focus of the original settlement.[28] This has not gone uncontested, since the layout of the later Norman walled town certainly looks as if it had Anglo-Saxon origins since its layout accords with similar examples from other parts of England where Anglo-Saxon origins are not in doubt.[29] The reality may have been that Anglo-Saxon Bristol had two original nuclei and that one developed into the later Norman walled town, while the other was superseded by the Norman castle. The settlement outside the later walls may in fact have grown up around an earlier *minster* church, that of St Peter, which by the twelfth century (*c.* 1150) was described by the bishop of Worcester as the foremost church in Bristol. Its status as a *minster* is fairly certain from the fact that it was mother-church of Mangotsfield, some five and a half miles away, and at *Domesday Book* held land amounting to three *hides*. This constituted fifty per cent of the land-holding of the manor of Barton Regis. By 1066, Barton Regis was a royal manor and held by King Harold II Godwinson.[30] There is therefore a strong likelihood that the *minster* of St Peter's was one of those eighth-century Mercian foundations identified in Chapter 4. This may help explain why a later defended settlement grew up at this spot, although the evidence is frustratingly thin for exactly when this occurred.

The likely early history of Anglo-Saxon Bristol therefore would see it as originally a settlement that grew up around the eighth-century Mercian church at St Peter's. Situated in a defensible point in the landscape, in a loop in the river Frome before this tributary flowed into the Avon, the site was further enhanced by the fact that it occupied well drained, elevated land. The easily defended nature of the site was even more apparent before the rerouting of the Frome, in 1247, which both greatly expanded the settlement area and also included much lower-lying land in the so-called 'Marsh'. The original site, on its elevated neck of land, also dominated the lowest bridging point on the river Avon. It was this which gave rise to its name, first recorded in 1051 in the *Chronicle*, of *Brycgstow*: 'Bridge-place'. This complex history probably created a bi-focal settlement with one focus around St Peter's and another just to the west at the bridging point. This assumes that the original Bristol Bridge was roughly where the current bridge is located; a point not beyond debate since a location a little to the east is also possible. The evidence from the Finzels Reach site suggests that this later bridge-point settlement may have been in place by the late tenth century. Whether this was related in any way to the earlier defensive activities along the Avon under Edward the Elder or, instead, started later in the tenth century is, as we have seen, difficult to say. However, it is possible that it had been a site of Edwardian activity, as at Bath. The *Chronicle* entry for 918 (see below) certainly shows that the Avon figured large in Edward's defensive priorities and the Bath evidence reinforces this. If it was under Edward the Elder that the original bridge was constructed, then it should probably be seen as enhancing his defensive activities since it would have blocked access up the Avon to any Viking fleet seeking to use the high tide. The Franks had used such tactics and Edward's father, Alfred, had also done so in 895 when a Viking fleet had sailed up the Thames and Lea and camped twenty miles north of London and were threatening the city. Alfred had then personally supervised the construction of a linked set of fortresses which created a fortified bridge of the kind built by the Franks. The end result was the trapping of the Viking ships further up the river Lea. Aware of this danger, the Viking army was forced to abandon its ships, send their families to East Anglia and then shifted their base westward, to Bridgenorth on the Severn. Alfred's system of defended *burhs*, the continuous availability of the revised local levies (the *fyrd*), and the use of the defended-bridge-strategy had triumphed. It is likely that Edward used similar strategies and Bristol *may* have been the site of one of these defended-bridges. If so, it followed the Frankish strategy of denying river-based access to Viking fleets, whereas Alfred's actions on the river Lea had trapped a Viking fleet which had already penetrated inland. Even if the building of the bridge at Bristol was not done under Edward the Elder, it is likely that it performed a similar function under a later king, perhaps Æthelred II. It seems clear that, by the year 1000, a defended settlement existed at Bristol. The Finzels Reach site ditch certainly seems to have existed at this date and tentatively dated finds of a similar period were unearthed in excavations at St Mary le Port, north of the Avon. Less easily dated defensive features appeared in excavations at Tower Street where a bank and ditch seems to have been in place by the eleventh century (along with the industrial activity mentioned earlier). Stray finds from the Castle site and Peter Street also suggest settlement by *c.* 1000.

If the bridgehead ditch was originally dug at an early date, then Bristol would have completed the line of defences along a long river frontier which united the rivers Avon and Thames. The *burghal* system would thus have run: (Bristol?), Bath, Malmesbury, Cricklade, Oxford, Wallingford, Sashes, and Southwark. If the defensive work at Bristol occurred later, then this suggests a late tenth-century extension of the system. Whatever the situation at Bristol, it is clear that, *c.* 910, the Avon was considered a frontier along its entire course; with the proviso that the frontier had looped north to include Bath. Furthermore, the *Chronicle* entry for 918 recorded Edward the Elder's orders for the guarding of the southern shores of the Severn estuary, 'from the west, from Cornwall, east as far as Avonmouth.'[31] That this coastal defence ended here clearly indicates that the line of the Avon continued to act as a demarcation of Edward's primary zone of activity, even given Viking raids further up the course of the Severn within this same *Chronicle* entry. Clearly, for the period of the Viking Wars (until at least the compilation of the *Burghal Hidage* document and probably a decade later) the river Avon was considered as a frontier along its entire course, with strategic military defended sites situated along its length. In fact, *Æthelweard's Chronicle* suggests that, depite evidence for the Avon declining in its frontier role by the late tenth century when he wrote, enough of a frontier association still survived for him to retrospectively describe an event of *c.* 910 in these words: 'After a year the barbarians [Vikings] broke the peace with King Edward, and with Æthelred, who then ruled the Northumbrian and Mercian areas. The fields of the Mercians were ravaged on all sides by the throng we spoke about, and deeply, as far as the streams of the Avon, where the boundary of the West Saxons and Mercians begins'.[32] This event also reveals that as late as 910 the Avon valley was still vulnerable to a long-range Viking raid.

Importantly, the *Burghal Hidage* also shows Bath as an integral part of the West Saxon kingdom and no longer a disputed area. It seems almost certain that sometime after the demise of Ceolwulf II – the last independent Mercian king, in 879 – Bath was finally absorbed into Wessex. The *Mercian Regnal List* gives Ceolwulf II a reign of 874–9 and states that by 883 Mercia was under the control of *Ealdorman* Æthelred, Alfred's son-in-law.[33] It is possible that

Ceolwulf II had a slightly longer reign, since his reign in the *Mercian Regnal List* may be rather short compared with the evidence for the fine silver coins minted in his name and also in association with Alfred. Therefore, Ceolwulf II may have reigned until he was superseded by *Ealdorman Æthelred* in 883.[34] It was clearly sometime after this date that Bath finally passed from the control of the Mercians and became a West Saxon town. After Burgred of Mercia granted a charter while staying in Bath in 864 there is no more mention of Bath with regard to Mercia and, despite the fact that it lay north of the Avon, it became absorbed into the county of Somerset and the Church diocese of Wells.

The *Anglo-Saxon Chronicle* implies that, by 906, the town of Bath had been annexed into Somerset and Wessex. The *Chronicle* annal for that year reads: 'In this year Alfred, who was reeve at Bath, died.'[35] This, otherwise unknown, Alfred was clearly of very significant interest to the West Saxon compiler of the *Chronicle*. It is therefore reasonable to assume that he was the first West Saxon royal official in the newly annexed territory. This suggests a fairly *recent* annexation and not one that had occurred under King Alfred in the late 870s, as has been suggested.[36] Two coins offer important corroborative evidence for the probable dating of this historic annexation of Bath into Wessex.[37]

Two Rare Coins of Edward the Elder that Point towards the Date of the Annexation of Bath by Wessex

Evidence that the West Saxon annexation of Bath, occurred prior to the reeve's death in 906, comes from the fact that Edward the Elder (ruled 899–924) was operating a mint there early in his reign. The evidence for this survives in the form of the unique Bath penny of Edward the Elder, which is now held in the British Museum.[38] This coin was minted before the year *c.* 905, because it was at this point, or very shortly afterwards, buried in what is known as the Cuerdale Hoard.[39] This was a Viking hoard of coins and cut-silver buried on the bank of the river Ribble in Lancashire. This focuses the 'date-window' for Bath's annexation into Wessex to *c.* 900–905. This is because Edward did not become king of Wessex until after his father's death, in October 899. Furthermore, he was actively engaged in putting down a challenge, by his cousin, Æthelwold, to his rule during that first winter of his reign (899–900) which was a serious revolt. Æthelwold was the son of a previous king of Wessex (one of Alfred's older brothers) and so reckoned that he had a better claim to the throne than did Alfred's son, Edward. As a result of this revolt, the year 900 is the earliest likely date for a significant action by Edward at Bath. A date after 902 (or even 903) may be even more likely. This is due to the fact that it was then that Æthelwold was killed in battle and his threat to Edward ended. Æthelwold had allied himself with the Vikings of Northumbria and of East Anglia and so threatened to overturn all that Alfred had achieved and passed on to his son.

The striking characteristics of this coin strongly suggest that the annexation of Bath took place in the early years of the reign of Edward the Elder. The Bath coin is unusual in a number of ways; the first of which is that it is the earliest example of any coin definitely minted at Bath. To be fair, this does not prove that this was the first time coins were ever issued from Bath. This needs to be considered since, in the late ninth and early tenth centuries, mint names are exceptional. As a result, we cannot assume that we now know all the mints which were operating at the time. A further relevant point, which encourages caution is that coins (bearing mint names) from Bath, Exeter and Winchester are all so rare that there are severe limits as to what we can say about the running and output of these mints. Despite these reservations, Bath's mint-signed coinage was from one of a West Saxon group from mints which had not been clearly active before. This fact may reinforce the view that minting probably began at Bath with this issue of Edward the Elder. An even more significant point, is that the coin carries the mint name on the reverse. This reads: 'BAÐ' (Bath). No other coin of Edward the Elder bears a mint name,[40] except for one where the mint name reads 'BA', and which is now in the Fitzwilliam Museum, Cambridge.[41] This was almost certainly also minted at Bath since no other mint operating at this time is identifiable from the 'BA' mint signature. Also, its style suggests that it dates from the same early period of Edward's reign. Its provenance is unclear and so, unlike the British Museum example from the Cuerdale Hoard, is less valuable for the task of tying down when the coin was minted. There is a possibility that it too originally came from Cuerdale but this cannot be proved.

These coins, therefore, stand out from all the rest of the coins minted under Edward the Elder. This makes them very important pieces of evidence indeed. Their character suggests that they represent a specific commemorative, or celebratory, issue and it seems very likely that this was Bath's new status as a West Saxon town.[42] Furthermore, Bath may also have become a fortified *burh* at about this time, although it is difficult to date the Late Saxon defences of the town. The Roman city wall of *Aquae Sulis*, on the northern side, survived into the Late Saxon period, when additional defences were dug on the edge of the Roman ditch, which was re-cut.[43] Bath shared this relationship between its Anglo-Saxon defences and surviving Roman walls with a number of towns in southern England.[44] Bath's defensive perimeter, as measured by the *Burghal Hidage*, appears calculated from these extended defences. The defences referred to in the *Burghal Hidage* were not necessarily newly built. However most Anglo-Saxon towns which restored old Roman walls seem to have done so in the tenth century.[45] All this suggests that the defences of Bath – as currently known – were the products of a building project of the late ninth, or early tenth century. In 2007, an impressive east-west orientated ditch to the south of the town wall was excavated during large-scale building work at the South Gate Development. This looks very much like being either the remains of the Roman defences which were cleared in the Late Saxon period, or a newly dug defensive ditch constructed as part of Alfred's or Edward's refortification of Bath. Exact dating, though, has not been established, so a definitive conclusion has not yet been reached regarding when this construction occurred.[46]

The surviving Roman walls – in whatever state of repair – may already have encouraged the use of Bath as a stronghold by Offa in the eighth century. So, while the completion of *burghal* defences may have prompted Edward the Elder to issue a celebratory coin, it might not have been the deciding factor behind this coin-issue as the walls may have been there already. Indeed, for Edward, the key factor may have been more that his pre-eminence in the Avon valley meant that the town was now open to West Saxon trade and taxation, which meant that the king's reeve could oversee economic transactions in Bath. This is particularly significant given the title of 'Alfred, who was reeve at Bath'. As the royal reeve, he was the one organising royal economic privileges in the town.

So, rebuilding the walls might not have been the only reason for producing such unusual coins. They might also have been minted to celebrate a royal visit to Bath or a major gift to the church there. We should never underestimate the importance of these Anglo-Saxon *minsters*, since they often were there long before fortified towns and trading settlements grew up around them.[47] This combined function of *minsters* and fortified sites had been a marked characteristic of Mercia before the Viking Wars and was one that later developed in Wessex too. In fact, about two-thirds of the settlements that were recorded in the *Burghal Hidage* either contained *minsters* or were situated close to a *minster*. As a consequence, it may have been that the very unusual Bath coins of Edward the Elder were minted because of the importance of the church at Bath. Frustratingly we do not know a great deal about the religious establishment at Bath, *c.* 900 but it has left some evidence for its, now lost, structures. A cross survives from north of the abbey,[48] and another from south of the present church's location.[49] This latter cross may date from the seventh century and may be a relic of the church established then by the rulers of the Hwicce (see Chapter 4). Burials have also been found in the south-eastern corner of what had once been the precinct of the Roman temple of Sulis-Minerva and some of these may date from the early eighth century.[50] However, even if the cause of minting the Bath pennies of Edward the Elder was linked to his support of the church at Bath, rather than the first rebuilding of the town's walls, this almost certainly was also combined with celebrating the West Saxon annexation of the once-Mercian border town, which would have had profound political as well as religious significance. We have seen how the spiritual and the political mixed in the competing activities of Anglo-Saxon kings along the Avon valley, as elsewhere in England.

This connection of the Bath pennies with an important church may be particularly important since in key features they resemble earlier coins of Alfred produced at Winchester and Exeter which were also major church centres. In fact it is surely significant that the Edward the Elder Bath penny in the British Museum has its closest parallels with coins of Alfred which also carry the mint-name as a three-letter statement: from Winchester, '*WIN*',[51] and from Exeter, '*EXA*'.[52] These coins also carry the royal title '*REX SAXONVM*' (king of the Saxons), and this royal title in this form is found only on Alfred's coins from these two mints.[53] This is all the more important because the Bath penny of Edward the Elder also carries the obverse title of '*+EADVVEARD REX SAXONVM*' (Edward king of the Saxons). Of all Edward's coins, only the ones from Bath (both the one in the British Museum and the one in the Fitzwilliam Museum) carry this title. Every other coin minted under Edward the Elder carries the royal title '*+EADVVEARD REX*' (Edward king). As a result, these two coins stand out from all Edward's other coins.[54] Clearly, Edward was trying to make a point; but what was it? What was the political message encoded in this title used exclusively on his Bath pennies?

The Power of Words – Why Edward Chose the Title that he Did on His Bath Pennies.

The large majority of Alfred's and Edward's coins simply give them the title '*REX*' (king). In contrast, '*REX SAXONVM*' (when it was used) was the title used by West Saxon kings in charters and on coins to express their role as kings of Wessex. It was occasionally used on coins during the reigns of Ecgbert and Æthelwulf earlier in the ninth century;[55] and Alfred and Edward occasionally used it. Its use was then revived later, in the tenth century. The use of this title of '*REX SAXONVM*' can be contrasted with the title '*Anglorum Saxonum rex*', or '*Angulsaxonum rex*' (king of the Anglo-Saxons) which developed in charters during Alfred's reign and was continued by Edward the Elder, to communicate a rule which now encompassed both Wessex and Mercia.[56] This was part of a new and expanded sense of the power of the kings of Wessex. The political message was clear on the Bath coins: although new titles expressed new and expanded West Saxon power, the title '*REX SAXONVM*' proclaimed the secure and settled power of the kings of the West Saxons within the traditional homeland of Wessex. Earlier Alfred had used this same royal title, with the reverse inscription '*ELI MO[sina]*', on a rare type of coin (by weight the equivalent of seven regular silver pennies) known to modern numismatists as 'Offering Pieces' because the reverse inscription probably meant 'alms/charitable donation'. These were probably intended as part of a ceremonial payment to the church in Rome or for some other charitable gift.[57] These 'Offering Pieces' were probably struck at Winchester late in Alfred's reign.[58] The use of the title '*REX SAXONVM*' on these coins further emphasises that it was used on special occasions to celebrate West Saxon identity. When it was used at Bath it clearly signalled that the town was now West Saxon. The message would not have been lost on literate viewers and users of these coins.

The title used on Edward the Elder's Bath pennies communicated the historic title of West Saxon monarchy and linked it with a tradition of ceremonial celebrations. The coins (with their unique mint name and West Saxon royal title) communicated the new political realities along the Avon valley and this was that Bath was now ruled by Edward, as king of Wessex. Even if the motivation for the issue of the Bath pennies was connected to a Church event rather than the rebuilding of the town walls, its political message was very clear. The days of Bath as a Mercian town were over. The 'western Avon' (which acted as a clear political boundary) would have an exception at Bath. Here the rule of Wessex would loop north to include this once-Mercian town. This anomaly would later be followed by the boundaries of the shire (Somerset) and Church boundaries.

This coin evidence reveals that the annexation of Bath into Wessex almost certainly occurred after 900 (when Edward the Elder was securely on the throne), or perhaps after 902 (the end of Æthelwold's revolt), and definitely by 906 (before the death of Alfred, 'reeve at Bath' and by when the Bath penny in the British Museum had been minted). These coins are therefore a very important part of the Avon valley story.

And a Final Clue...

Despite this annexation into Wessex *c.* 905, the position of Bath still seemed to be ambiguous and this sense lingered to the end of the Anglo-Saxon period of history. Under the *Domesday Book* entry for Wiltshire, in 1086, the king is quoted as having 'the third penny' from: Salisbury, Marlborough, Cricklade, Bath and Malmesbury.[59] The 'third penny' was the profits from justice in a shire or town. This was the result of many crimes being punished by a fine. In a town this was usually split so that the king received two pennies in every three pennies levied as fines, while the 'third penny' went to the earl (the regional nobility under the king).[60] In the case of these five towns, though, it was the 'third penny' (a reduced amount) that went to the king. What is intriguing, though, is that all these towns are in Wiltshire *except* Bath. It seems

One of the sources of the river Avon at Cherry Orchard, just within the Wiltshire border by Badminton Park.

One of the sources of the river Avon at Crow Down Springs, near Sherston. *Æthelweard's Chronicle* refers to 'the streams [or springs] of the Avon, where the boundary of the West Saxons and Mercians begins'.

Pub sign of the Rattlebone Inn, Sherston. It commemorates the local legend of John Rattlebone, said to have fought alongside Edmund Ironside, against Cnut at the battle of Sherston, 1016. *By permission of the proprietor of The Rattlebone Inn.*

River Avon at Sherston.

Malmesbury Abbey, contested by Wessex and Mercia.

14th century effigy, commemorating Athelstan's burial in Malmesbury Abbey. *By permission of the Vicar and Churchwardens of Malmesbury Abbey.*

St Andrew's church, Chippenham. The West Saxon royal estate-centre, captured by Vikings in 878, would have been in the vicinity.

Westbury White Horse. Alfred defeated the Vikings near here in 878.

River Avon at Lacock, where it flows through the Avon Vale.

Church of St Michael and All Angels, Melksham. On the site of an Anglo-Saxon *minster*.

River Avon at Bradford on Avon, Town Bridge.

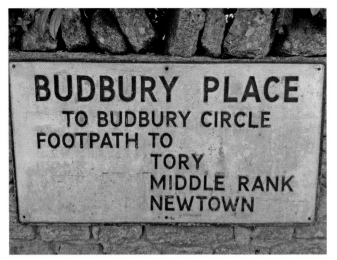

Only the street-names survive of Budbury hillfort, Bradford on Avon. Almost certainly the location of 'Vortigern's Fort' and a battle in 652.

Excavation at Budbury Manor has revealed the ditch of the Iron Age hillfort.
By permission of Roy Canham.

Bradford on Avon: Holy Trinity church (on site of the *minster*) to the left and 'Saxon Church' of St Laurence in the centre.

St Laurence church was almost certainly built as a refuge for the relics of Edward King and Martyr, *c*.1001.

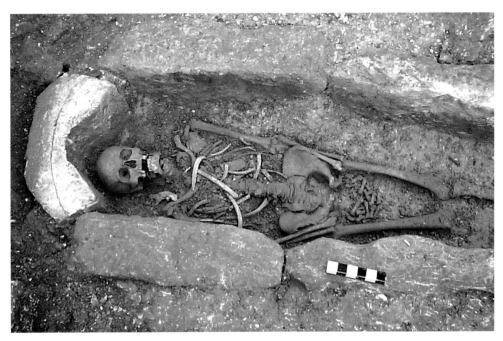

Anglo-Saxon cist burial discovered near St Laurence church, at Glebe Cottage. Probably contemporary with the 'Saxon Church'. *By permission of Adrian Powell.*

The size of the 14th century Tithe Barn at Bradford on Avon is indicative of the wealth of the estate granted to Shaftesbury Abbey in 1001.

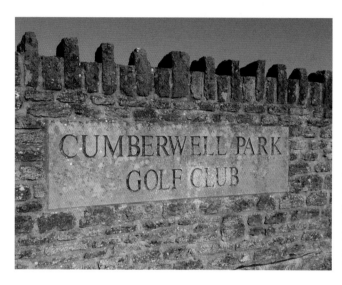

The place-name Cumberwell reveals the survival of a British community near Bradford on Avon after the area was conquered by Wessex.

Place-names north-west of Bradford on Avon reveal a well wooded past.

Avon valley at Barton Country Park, Bradford on Avon.

In the vicinity of Avoncliff, the river Avon enters the Limpley Stoke Valley.

The Limpley Stoke Valley: an historic dividing point on the Avon's course.

View towards Solsbury Hill, near Bath. A possible location of the battle of Badon.

View towards Hinton Camp, possible location of the battle of Dyrham, AD 577.

Commanding view from Hinton Camp towards the river Severn and Wales.

Bath Abbey, once a *minster* of the Hwicce and later of Mercia; and closely associated with the Mercian royal family.

Bath penny of Edward the Elder. Reverse reads: *BA* (Bath). Minted *c.* 900-905. *Copyright The Fitzwilliam Museum*

Bath penny of Edward the Elder. Obverse reads: *EADVVEARD REX SAXONVM* (Edward king of the Saxons). Minted *c.* 900-905. *Copyright The Fitzwilliam Museum*

The West Wansdyke, north side and looking eastward towards Englishcombe.

A wooded hilltop conceals Stantonbury hillfort, which lies on the line of the West Wansdyke.

Site of Keynsham Abbey, location of an earlier *minster* church and burial place of Heahmund, bishop of Sherborne, in 871.

Anglo-Saxon sculpture, found on the site of Keynsham Abbey and reused in a later wall. *By permission of Charles Gerrish.*

View towards Bristol Bridge, viewed from the Mercian side of the river Avon.

View towards Frinzels Reach and the location of the defended bridgehead of Anglo-Saxon Bristol on the south bank of the river Avon.

St Peter's church, Bristol. Probably one of the chain of Mercian *minsters* on the Avon's north bank. A view eastward past St Peter's Church towards Castle Park and the probable location of Anglo-Saxon Bristol.

The medieval crossroads of Bristol, a pattern which may point towards an earlier Anglo-Saxon arrangement of streets.

At Clifton Gorge the Avon cuts through dramatic scenery on its way to the sea at Avonmouth.

The Gokstad Ship, Viking Ship Museum Oslo. Unearthed in 1880, it is the kind of ship that would have brought Scandinavians to England and whose movements up the river Avon a fortified Bristol Bridge would have prevented.

strange that it should have been attached to a Wiltshire list by the *Domesday* commissioners and not one for Somerset. This may suggest that Bath was an anomaly and was not always counted as part of Somerset and, as such, this might be a faint echo of when it was not in Somerset. This means that, while Bath was fully absorbed into Wessex by 906, its position in Somerset was recognised as being rather irregular, given that the rest of Somerset's northern boundary ran (and still runs) along the line of the 'western Avon'. In some ways it might have made even more sense if Bath had been associated in *Domesday Book* with administrative arrangements for Gloucestershire in this respect, since this was old Mercian territory. Nevertheless, the eleventh-century 'third penny' evidence clearly points out the unusual status and position of Bath as late as 1086. It may even – and this is highly speculative – have been based on echoes of even older administrative arrangements dating to the Roman period (as identified by Ptolemy in Chapter 2), when the Bath region was administered from far to the east.

Another Avon Valley Refuge-Place

Recent research has identified a number of potential refuges for civilians and animals during periods of warfare and dating from the eighth or ninth century in north-western Wiltshire. This research suggests that Bradford on Avon – along with Great Bedwyn – shows evidence for 'royal estates corresponding to *minster parochiae* [areas served by a major church] emerging with centres in close proximity to Iron Age hillforts at Budbury and Chisbury respectively'.[61] A similar pattern can be discerned at Avebury. The *minster* church at Bradford is likely to have been on the site of the later Norman church of Holy Trinity and was probably in existence by the early eighth century judging from stone sculptural finds in the vicinity. Over the course of the ninth century a network of defensible places began to emerge in Wessex and it seems that Bradford on Avon was one of a series of refuges based around an Iron Age hillfort, a royal estate and a *minster*. This research is intriguing as it suggests that a network of local 'refuge-places' existed beyond those larger places recorded as *burhs*. Operating below the 'radar of the *Burghal Hidage*', they do not appear in contemporary records of defended places but would have played an important role in local defence and in the protection of civilians and portable wealth. That Budbury had earlier appeared as 'Vortigern's fort' in a seventh-century context adds weight to the significance of this hillfort above the river-cliff at Bradford on Avon.

The Avon Valley by the Death of Edward the Elder.

By the time that Edward the Elder died, in 924, the situation along the Avon valley frontier had changed dramatically since the start of the Viking Wars in the previous century. No longer was it a boundary between kingdoms. Indeed, no longer was it even contested between kingdoms. The old Mercia had gone and West Saxon rule extended far to the north. In 919, following the death of his sister, Æthelflæd the Lady of the Mercians, Edward had acted swiftly to end Mercian independence and to bring it fully under West Saxon control. In 920 the Northumbrians, the Scots and the Strathclyde Welsh submitted to Edward. Earlier, in 918, the Welsh kings had submitted to him. This followed on from a decade in which he had – first in alliance with Æthelflæd and Æthelred her husband and then, following Æthelred's death, in alliance with Æthelflæd alone – conquered the East Midland *Danelaw* territories previous lost to Viking rule. Consequently, by his death Edward had presided over the conquest of the *Danelaw*, the annexation of Mercia and had been accepted as overlord by all the other kings and rulers in Britain. It was a considerable achievement and it changed the whole balance of power along the Avon, as indeed throughout the whole of England south of the river Humber and even beyond it. As a result of these actions, the Avon was finally a river flowing *within* the territory of just one Anglo-Saxon kingdom; and that kingdom was well on the way to becoming the sole kingdom in and of 'England'; a role finally achieved in 954 on the death of Eric Bloodaxe, the last Viking king of York.

This process has started in the reign of Alfred, since Mercia had had no king after the death of Ceolwulf II in 879. Western Mercia (all that remained outside Scandinavian control) was thereafter ruled by Alfred's son-in-law, Æthelred, and his daughter, Æthelflæd, as the Lord and Lady of the Mercians. However, they were not monarchs and ruled as junior partners of Alfred. A joint Wessex-Mercia kingdom of the 'Anglo-Saxons' emerged out of this unequal arrangement. Nevertheless, within this period, a rump Mercia undoubtedly continued to have its historic southern border with Wessex along the 'western Avon'. Where the frontier lay east of Bath is less obvious given the ambiguous nature of the 'eastern Avon' as a political boundary and the limited nature of the surviving documentary evidence. All this changed in 919 due to the decisive action of Edward the Elder; and the Bath region had already had a foretaste of his annexations in the previous decade.

At this point in the tenth century it must have seemed clear that the future of the Avon lay solely as an administrative boundary within the emerging kingdom of England. It would clearly be a matter of shire and diocesan borders which would decide its future role; its function as a kingdom frontier was over. However, reality proved to be more complex. Events in the later tenth and early eleventh centuries would once again have repercussions along the valley of the Avon.

CHAPTER 6

A Fluctuating Frontier in an Increasingly United England

The reign of Athelstan (924–939) continued the unity of Wessex and Mercia but, at the start and especially at the end of his reign, the old kingdom boundary of the river Avon was once more in the political spotlight. This illustrates the way in which Anglo-Saxon political relationships were still being negotiated along the Avon valley and in the south-west Midlands generally. Even an event such as the coronation of Edgar at Bath in 973, supposedly symbolic of the new unity of England, can be seen to have still been part of this process of negotiation that reflected a consciousness of earlier boundaries. In addition, at key points within the tenth and eleventh centuries the Avon valley again became a frontier zone between kingdoms at times of political stress (under kings Eadwig and Edgar and later in the new phase of Viking conflict between Cnut and Edmund Ironside). How these political crises led to this re-emergence will be considered in this chapter, along with the way in which the emerging diocesan and shire boundaries grew out of an earlier kingdom frontier.

After the reign of Edward the Elder and the West Saxon conquest of the *Danelaw* under Edward and his sister, Æthelflæd, it appeared that the function of the Avon as a kingdom frontier was over. A characteristic that had begun with the British successor states in the fifth century and then the Anglo-Saxon kingdoms in the sixth and seventh centuries had finally been superseded by the union of Wessex and Mercia in 919 and then by the creation of a united kingdom of England under Edward's son, Athelstan and his successors. Athelstan's reign would see a West Saxon king annex Viking Northumbria, invade Scotland and finally defeat a huge alliance of enemies: Vikings, Scots and Welsh at the battle of *Brunanburh* in 937. A new royal title of *REX TO (tius) BRIT (anniae)* – King of all Britain – appeared on Athelstan's coinage, along with the first illustration of any English monarch wearing a crown. However, the longevity of old traditions combined with the fragility of the new political arrangements to ensure that this was by no means a permanent state.

A Brief Re-emergence of an Old Frontier

When Edward the Elder died, in 924, there was immediately something of a political crisis in his newly formed 'Anglo-Saxon' kingdom. Athelstan, his son, had been raised in Mercia in the household of his aunt, Æthelflæd, the Lady of the Mercians and her husband Æthelred, Lord of Mercia. This was almost certainly part of a deliberate policy by Edward to encourage Mercian acceptance of West Saxon overlordship. One of its legacies was that Athelstan was always something of an outsider amongst the West Saxon elites and, as we shall shortly see, his selection of burial place clearly indicated that he was aware of this and emphasises the importance of the Avon valley frontier.

Consequently, the succession proved to be anything but straightforward. Despite being the eldest son of Edward the Elder, Athelstan's succession to the throne was threatened by the existence of a younger half-brother, Ælfweard, who had been born to Edward's latest wife. A very much later account of Athelstan's boyhood, the *Gesta regum Anglorum* (*Deeds of the Kings of the English*), written by William of Malmesbury in the early twelfth century, claimed that Edward the Elder had named Athelstan as his heir. In addition, Athelstan's grandfather, Alfred, had recognised his throne-worthiness with a gift of a scarlet cloak, a jewelled belt and a richly decorated sword. Despite this, Athelstan's succession was anything but secure.

As a result of this sibling rivalry, when Edward died in July, 924, his newly unified kingdom looked set to disintegrate. How far this was what Edward intended we cannot now tell. The sources are simply too sparse. It may have been that he actually intended that Ælfweard would inherit the entire kingdom. Alternatively, he may have intended to divide his newly united kingdom. This is certainly what actually happened. However, the division that followed may not have been due to any prearranged plan.[1] In the *Anglo-Saxon Chronicle*, the *manuscript A* (the oldest surviving version) records the death of Edward and the accession of Athelstan. However, the *Mercian Register* gives a much fuller account. Given Athelstan's Mercian upbringing this is not surprising. This states that Athelstan was chosen as king by the Mercians. In the context of the Avon valley, this would have revived a frontier arrangement that appeared buried in 919. We do not know where the old Mercian/West Saxon boundary lay on the 'eastern Avon' but on the 'western Avon' it clearly followed the river from Bath (newly annexed into Wessex) to the mouth of the Avon. A kingdom frontier had suddenly reappeared, along this length of the river's course at least.

The reappearance though was only a fleeting one. This was because Athelstan soon added the crown of Wessex to his Mercian authority. However, he only succeeded to Wessex as well because his half-brother, Ælfweard, died 'very soon after' Edward the Elder.[2] Another manuscript of the *Chronicle* (*manuscript D*, the so-called *Worcester Chronicle*) states that Ælfweard outlived his father by just sixteen days. In which case the reappearance of the Avon as a kingdom boundary was brief indeed! Had he lived, it seems likely that he would have ruled Wessex. Mercia then would have been taken by Athelstan.

Athelstan was not crowned until September, 925. This suggests that he was seen as something of an outsider by the Winchester elite and had to overcome opposition. That he was aware of this is evident from two events connected to the border monastery of Malmesbury. In each case, Athelstan's devotion to the monastery and its patron saint, Aldhelm, was almost certainly because it lay in a frontier zone long contested by Wessex and Mercia. As such it was located well away from the traditional West Saxon centre of gravity at Winchester and could be spiritually claimed for both Mercia and Wessex.

Athelstan and the Abbey at Malmesbury.

Regarding Athelstan's victory at *Brunanburh*, in 937, William of Malmesbury, writing in the early twelfth century, records how Athelstan, faced with the likelihood of a Viking victory, cries out to God and to St Aldhelm to assist him. At this point a miraculous sword appears in his scabbard. With this he inflicts a crushing defeat on the Vikings and their allies. Now it is clear that William was determined to promote the fame of Aldhelm because he was closely associated with William's monastic house of Malmesbury.[3] However, this was more convincing because he knew that Athelstan was indeed very closely connected with the monastery on the river Avon. This was because when Athelstan died, two years later in Gloucester, he was buried at the border monastery of Malmesbury in the frontier zone between Wessex and Mercia.[4] According to William of Malmesbury, the monastery had earlier benefitted from the patronage of the king. He had given Malmesbury many gifts of land and holy relics.

There had, indeed, been many gifts of land to Malmesbury and the urban *burh* now located there (see Chapter 5). In 939 he had granted five *hides*, near Norton (Wiltshire), to the townspeople (*burgesses*) at Malmesbury.[5] In 931, Athelstan granted to the church of Malmesbury 5 hides, again at Norton (Wiltshire), 5 *hides* at *Sumerford* (probably Little Somerford, Wiltshire) and 5 *hides* at Ewen (Gloucestershire).[6] This estate had an interesting back-story since it had earlier been forfeited by a nobleman, named Alfred, for conspiracy. This almost certainly referred back to an event in the ninth-century Viking Wars. In 937, the king was particularly generous in his bequests to Malmesbury. In that one year alone he granted the abbey: 60 *hides* at Bremhill (Wiltshire);[7] 10 *hides* at Wootton (Wiltshire);[8] and finally a massive set of 10 *hides* at Wootton, 60 *hides* at Bremhill, 5 *hides* at *Sumerford* (again probably Little Somerford), 5 *hides* at Norton, (all Wiltshire) and 5 *hides* at Ewen (Gloucestershire).[9] These grants certainly corroborate William of Malmesbury's account and reveal the extent of Athelstan's devotion to this frontier abbey.

In contrast, he was far less generous to Bath. In 931 Athelstan granted to the monastery of St Peter's, Bath 10 *hides* at Priston (Somerset) and 5 *hides* at Cold Ashton, (Gloucestershire). As with the grant to Malmesbury of land at Ewen, this estate too had been forfeited by the nobleman Alfred, for conspiracy.[10] That is it; no other records of land granted to Bath exist and it is clear that the king did not have the close affinity with this particular monastery, compared with his relationship with that at Malmesbury.

Royal interest in the Avon valley continued into the 940s but the evidence does not reveal the same degree of information that can be deduced from the earlier grants to the churches at Malmesbury and at Bath. Athelstan had not married and was succeeded by his brother, Edmund. In 941, King Edmund granted to Æthelnoth, *minister* (nobleman), 10 *hides* at Corston (Somerset).[11] In 946 the grant is a little more revealing and may suggest the wish to have especially loyal followers in this once-sensitive area. In that year, Edmund granted to Æthelhere, his faithful *minister*, 5 *hides* at Weston, near Bath, on the condition that he and his heirs remained faithful to Edmund until the king's death. Thereafter, they were to transfer their loyalty to a designated friend (*amicus* in Latin) of the king.[12] On its own this might not seem to signify a great deal. However, a whole flurry of land grants in the vicinity of Bath in the 950s indicates that the Bath region had suddenly become a politically sensitive area.

A Kingdom Frontier Yet Again ... the Peculiar Land Grants of King Eadwig.

In 946, King Edmund died. He was murdered at Pucklechurch (Gloucestershire) while attempting to save one of his *thegns* (noblemen) from a robber. He was buried at Glastonbury and was succeeded by his brother, Eadred.

In 955, Eadred too died, at Frome, in Somerset. He was succeeded by his nephews. These were the sons of Edmund his brother (the one murdered, in 946, at Pucklechurch). These two brothers – Eadwig (or Edwy) and Edgar – for a short time divided the recently united kingdom between them. Once more the Avon became a kingdom frontier (at least on its western course), as Mercia and Wessex again seemed set to separate into autonomous kingdoms. This did not happen immediately. At first, Eadwig inherited a united kingdom from Eadred. However, there were clearly divisions within the royal household with some nobles backing Eadwig, while others supported Edgar. This is clear because, in 957, Edgar succeeded to the kingdom of Mercia. The *Anglo-Saxon*

Chronicle, in *manuscript D*, dates this to 955; *manuscripts B* and *C* indicate 957 as the year when Edgar came to the throne in Mercia and the later date best fits the available evidence. Consequently, England was divided along the river Thames (and also along the line of the Bristol Avon). The river Thames is specified as the frontier in the period of division;[13] but this reference does not define the boundary west of the upper Thames and for this the earlier kingdom boundaries are the most plausible. While this division reflected internal political factions within the court it did not become a long lasting division because, in 959, Eadwig died. Consequently, the sixteen-year-old Edgar inherited the crown and so reunited the kingdom.

Prior to this, though, Eadwig (ruling 955–9) had been peculiarly active in granting land. The statistics speak for themselves. There are eighty-seven surviving charters for the reign of Eadwig and, of these, fifty-five are from a single year, 956, and these alone make up five per cent of the entire corpus of Anglo-Saxon charters. This is remarkable, to put it mildly, for a king who ruled for only four years. Given the relative paucity and seeming bias of the narrative sources for his reign (they do not like him) these charters can give a key insight into the reign of Eadwig and shed light on the tensions within the court and Church politics associated with him. Whether all the land granted in the charters was originally royal land, or was land that had been confiscated, or was reallocated Church land is not entirely clear. Interestingly, several of the charters issued in 956 were for tracts of land that had previously been granted in charters within the past twenty years; there was a tendency in the mid tenth century for land to be re-issued as kings maximised the potential benefits from a shrinking amount of available land (so much already being in the ownership of the Church).

The charters from 957 are subtly different in their style when compared to other charters of Eadwig and provide an insight into the division of the kingdom between Eadwig and his younger brother, Edgar, which occurred in 957, as the charters span the period of this division. The difference suggests that Eadwig was attempting to assert himself and develop an independent powerbase at a time when, in reality, his position was not fully secure. The narrative sources suggest that this division was due to civil war, while the charter evidence seems to point to a more amicable split. That the division was complex is clear from the numismatic evidence which seems to show Eadwig minting coins in Mercia until the end of his reign (despite this being Edgar's territory). In what sense then the kingdom was divided with Edgar is therefore a little unclear. Nevertheless, some kind of division did occur in 957; and in this critical period Eadwig became peculiarly focused on the Avon valley in the vicinity of Bath and Malmesbury.

There is corroborative evidence for this in the manner in which Eadwig took a noticeable interest in Bath, making grants to Bath in 956 and 957, specifically mentioning his priest, Wulfgar. That of 956 specified that the grant was to 'St Peter's Abbey, Bath, and to Wulfgar, abbot; grant of 30 *hides* at Tidenham [Gloucestershire], of which three are to belong to the abbot'.[14] That of 957 was more specific in its highlighting of Wulfgar as the beneficiary, as it was to 'St Peter's Abbey, Bath; at the request of his *sacerdos* [priest] Wulfgar, of ten *hides* at Bathford'.[15] That Wulfgar was Eadwig's man is clear from the description of him as being 'his priest'. Eadwig seems to have installed one of his royal priests as head of the *minster* at Bath, 'probably as a reward for his services but perhaps also in order to have one of his own men in charge of the principal church in a strategic town on the boundary between Wessex and Mercia'.[16] Such a man – experienced within the royal household and personally loyal to Eadwig – could be expected to represent Eadwig's interests in this section of the Avon valley.

In a similar way, in 956, he granted land at Bathampton Down (which dominated eastern Bath) to a man named Hehelm. The wording of this charter is particularly interesting: 'King Eadwig to Hehelm, his *fidelis*; grant of five *hides* at Bathampton [Somerset]', with a note that Hehelm promised the land to Bath Abbey after his death.[17] Calling Hehelm his '*fidelis*' (faithful/loyal servant) clearly indicates that he was a loyal supporter of Eadwig and the kind of man that Eadwig could trust at a time when the elites of Wessex and Mercia were sharply polarised in their competitive support for Eadwig or his brother, Edgar. The grant was carefully contrived so that it rewarded both the loyal Hehelm, as long as he lived, and then the loyal monastic community at Bath, when Hehelm eventually died. Other charters presented Eadwig as the righter of wrongs, in the favour of the community at Bath. One, of 956, described the grant as being a 'restitution of five *hides* at Weston', near Bath.[18] Another, of 959, promised the 'restoration of five *hides* at Olveston, and five at Cold Ashton [Gloucestershire], granted to the *minster* by King Athelstan'.[19] The references to 'restitution' and 'restoration' indicate that the monastery at Bath had somehow lost control of these estates. That was now rectified by Eadwig and the lost estates were returned to the community at Bath. No doubt they were grateful.

It is clear that Eadwig's grants were designed to win the support of local elites at this border town and also at Malmesbury, 'another *burh* lying between Wessex and Mercia', where he was a patron.[20] Here, evidence of a more favourable assessment of the king than is found in most surviving sources suggests he patronised this monastery which was 'once more on a strategic boundary'.[21] One of these charters granted to Malmesbury a huge estate of 100 *hides* at Brokenborough, (Wiltshire);[22] a grant reflected in another document (also preserved in the Malmesbury archive) which outlined the extent of the Malmesbury land there and also at Sutton Benger (Wiltshire).[23] The land at Brokenborough represented what had once been a major royal estate (a *villa regalis*), but it now passed from royal hands into that of the community at Malmesbury. It was a very generous gift and one that would have carried the clear message of royal favour. It was, no doubt, a favour that was hoped to be returned. In this brief period the significant number of land grants made by Eadwig to Bath and Malmesbury suggests he was reinforcing his position in what was, once more, a sensitive frontier zone. It was in these areas that land under his own authority abutted territory controlled by Edgar, his brother. Given the historic interest of Mercia in Bath, the donations there were almost certainly made in order to assert Eadwig's authority there and to remind the community at Bath that their best interests were now served by recognising the primacy of Wessex over Mercia. They were, it was clear, to see themselves as firmly within the camp of the former, despite their historic connections to the latter.

After the death of Eadwig, in 959, Edgar reunited Mercia with Wessex and a unified kingdom was once again restored. The *Anglo-Saxon Chronicle*, in *manuscripts B* and *C*, specifically emphasises the reunion of 'Wessex, Mercia and Northumbria' under one king. Like his brother, this powerful and astute king was more than capable of making the most of symbolic opportunities and in this royal attention once more turned to the Avon valley.

The Coronation of King Edgar at Bath: a Location Carefully Chosen

On Whitsunday, 973, Edgar was crowned at Bath and anointed alongside his wife, Ælfthryth. This great confirmation of his kingship actually occurred some fourteen years after he had reunited the two kingdoms under his sole rule. It marked not the commencement but, instead, the culmination of his reign. Occurring at a point in his life when he was about thirty years of age, there were clear parallels with the age at which Jesus Christ began his ministry and when he was baptised in the river Jordan, by John the Baptist. It is very possible that a work of Anglo-Saxon Church liturgy – *Æthelwold's Benedictional,* with its emphasis on Christ's kingship and baptism and a link drawn between baptismal anointing with oil (*chrism*) and a king's coronation – was produced for Edgar's coronation.[24] Clearly, Edgar was presenting himself as God's anointed ruler of England and making a definite statement about the sanctity of his royal position. That this was indeed the case is further emphasised by the fact that the coronation took place at Pentecost, when the gift of God's Holy Spirit was poured on the Church, as recorded in the Book of Acts, in the New Testament. This occasion drew attention to the divine empowering of Edgar and was also a traditional time for the celebration of Christian baptisms. The latter further emphasised both the new start in Edgar's kingship and the parallel being drawn with the opening of Christ's ministry at the river Jordan.

Later, Edgar's overlordship was recognised at Chester by neighbouring kings. These included the king of Scots, the British king of Strathclyde and the Viking ruler, Maccus Haraldsson, who ruled the Hebrides. [25] Edgar was rowed along the river Dee by eight kings. As they provided the motive power, Edgar took the tiller. The imagery was clear: he was guiding the political destiny of Britain.

The year 973 was clearly one charged with political significance and in this year of highly symbolic gestures, Bath was very much to the fore. The service that was used for the coronation of Edgar was compiled by Dunstan (St Dunstan), the archbishop of Canterbury. It has formed the basis of all subsequent coronation services, including that of Queen Elizabeth II, in 1953. For this alone the event would deserve its much honoured place in the constitutional and political history of England. It was in recognition of this that, in 1973, Queen Elizabeth II visited Bath Abbey for a service which marked the passage of one thousand years since the coronation of King Edgar. The 'Bath Monarchy 1000' event reminds us of the part that the Avon valley has played in English history. However, the event in 973 is even more significant for it was crafted to make a number of points, in addition to those already discussed. The choice of Bath can be seen to have held a twofold significance in these.

Firstly, it was an imperial city. Its Roman heritage was reflected in the imperial pretensions of Edgar. We do not know how much of the Roman structures of Bath were upstanding in 973 but there were undoubtedly sufficient of them to remind visitors of its past imperial grandeur. This is reflected in an Old English poem, *The Ruin*, which reflected on the evidence for past greatness at Bath. It was in Old English '*enta geweorc*', or 'the work of the Giants', which reminded those contemplating it of times when 'many a man mood-glad, goldbright ... gazed on wrought gemstones, on gold, on silver ...'[26] In its description of stone houses, hot streams contained within a stone wall and hot baths, it can surely only be describing Bath; although this is not actually specified in the actual poem. Although the poem reflects the way fate brought low the imperial city, it also reflects the manner in which *Romanitas* continued to cast a long shadow over Anglo-Saxon imaginations. It was this sense of being inheritors of – and restorers of – the past greatness of Rome that lay behind the choice of Bath as the location for the 973 coronation. The city of *The Ruin*, even in its broken state, was '*wrætlic*' (wondrous). If, in fact, *The Ruin* does describe Bath (and it is our definite contention that it does) then both its language and its date of composition is instructive. Recent study has shown that its forty-nine lines were composed using an Old English vocabulary that was largely Late West Saxon, but a number of its features point to an original place of composition outside of Wessex, possibly Mercia.[27] This would certainly be consistent with an awareness of the location and situation at Bath, with its Roman ruins, on the boundary of Wessex and Mercia. Furthermore, it is found in the tenth-century *Exeter Book*, although it may originally have been written as early as the eighth century. In short, it does not reflect a fifth century sub-Roman experience but, instead, a poetic perspective on the past from the age of Offa at the earliest. Alone of Old English poetry, it is concerned with a place and not a person.[28]

The location also connected with more contemporary reinventions of *Romanitas* in the Holy Roman Empire. It put Edgar on a par with rulers of the Frankish superpower across the channel. The great Charlemagne had undergone a double coronation in the eighth century; and in 962 the Emperor Otto the Great had been crowned in a ceremony which may have inspired Edgar to emulate it.[29] This is all the more likely because Otto had married Athelstan's sister and his imperial rites may already have influenced the earlier christening of Edgar's son, Edmund, in 966.[30] Earlier rulers had attempted similar emulation and had also chosen Bath as a place to achieve this. As we have seen, Offa of Mercia may have chosen Bath as a location for frontier actions because, like Charlemagne's palace complex at Aachen, it too was the site of a hot spring. This desire to be seen as the successors to Roman authority is revealed in the claim in Byrhtferth's late tenth-century *Vita Sancti Oswaldi* (*Life of St Oswald*) that, just prior to the coronation at Bath, Oswald (on returning from Rome) had brought Edgar the blessing of the pope.[31]

Secondly, Bath was an old frontier town. Consciously, or unconsciously, it had become part of the tradition of the West Saxon ascent to greatness that was ingrained within the story of the English monarchy by the latter half of the tenth century. The West Saxon annexation of the town had occasioned the only time that Edward the Elder had named a mint location on any of his coins and had declared his royal title in the traditional West Saxon formula (see Chapter 5). It was at Bath that Eadwig had concentrated a significant amount of land granting at a point in time when he was contesting the kingdom with Edgar. It was to Bath that Edgar came for his imperial coronation. The pattern is too significant to be coincidental. Bath mattered; and it mattered as much because it symbolised the triumph of the House of Wessex as because it was an imperial city. That it was *both*, made the location all the more attractive.

All of this was reflected in a poem found in the *Anglo-Saxon Chronicle* for 973. It emphasised the symbolic significance of Edgar's age, the timing of this royal ritual and the associations of Bath.[32] In a strange piece of inventiveness it even gave Bath a new name; one virtually unknown outside this poem and almost certainly invented in order to heighten the effect of the location at an old Roman settlement. The writer of the poem named Bath as: *Acemannesceaster*. It was, in the poem's Old English, '*on ðære ealdran byrig*' ('the ancient town'). The place name, *Acemannesceaster*, in place of the usual Old English name *Bað* (Bath) is certainly striking. It was possibly crafted so that it echoed aspects of both the Roman name *Aquae Sulis* and the name of the Frankish city of Aachen.[33] It is even more likely that it was derived from an Old English name for the stretch of Roman road linking Watling Street with the *Fosse Way* at Cirencester. This was known as 'Akeman Street' and the name may once have been used for part at least of the *Fosse Way* itself, which crosses the river Avon at Bath. Alternatively, it may actually really have been an alternative name for Bath; in which case the name may have meant 'the road to Bath'.[34] Whatever the case, its usage did not survive. Bath remained 'Bath'. But, in 973, the brief appearance of the place name *Acemannesceaster* further emphasised Bath's Roman credentials.

We do not know a great deal archaeologically about mid to late ninth-century Bath. A coin hoard, of fifty silver pennies, deposited *c.* 955 contained coins of Alfred to Eadred. This was discovered, still in a wooden box, in the burial ground of Abbey House.[35] Other, slight, evidence for Saxo-Norman occupation was discovered in trial excavations at Lambridge.[36] We would like to know more about the place that Edgar chose for his great coronation but, at present, the archaeology of Late Anglo-Saxon Bath remains hidden under the modern city.

Like Bath, Chippenham on the Avon also continued to be an important royal centre throughout the tenth century and, like Bath and Bradford on Avon, this probably owed something to its historic interest to West Saxon kings due to its earlier importance as being located in a frontier zone between Wessex and Mercia. Royal councils met there a number of times as revealed by charters that were witnessed while the king was resident there, such as Athelstan in 930 and 933,[37] and Edmund in 940.[38] In addition to these charters, an earlier document reveals that Edward the Elder was the recipient of a letter, written to him in 924, which referred to him spending time at Chippenham.[39]

In 975, Edgar died and was succeeded by his son, Edward. In 978, Edward (who was later known as 'Edward King and Martyr') was murdered at Corfe, in Dorset. He was succeeded by his half-brother. This was Æthelred II, who was later known as 'Æthelred *unræd* ', meaning 'without wisdom/counsel'. In 980, Viking raiders attacked Southampton, along with Thanet and Cheshire. A whole new chapter in the Viking Wars had started.

The Avon Valley in the Second Great Phase of the Viking Wars

At the death of King Edgar it seemed that, finally, the Avon's role as a kingdom frontier was over. It did, though, preserve echoes of its former importance. In 1001 King Æthelred II granted Bradford on Avon to the nuns of Shaftesbury

Abbey as a safe refuge for themselves and the relics of his half-brother Edward King and Martyr who had been murdered at Corfe in 978.

The selection of Bradford was significant. The fact that St Aldhelm (a member of the West Saxon royal family) had founded a church there *c.* 705 suggests that Bradford had been a royal estate since the seventh century and its next appearance in the written record supports that interpretation. The will of King Eadred, from 951–5, grants Bradford – along with two other estates – to Nunnaminster.[40] It seems likely that the *Bradanford* given to these nuns of Winchester in Eadred's will refers to the Wiltshire Bradford as the near-by Calne was also donated in the same will. However, none of the bequests made in Eadred's will seem to have been followed through and his successors appear to have deliberately gone against his wishes. By 1066 five of these nine estates still belonged to the crown and three of them were held by different religious houses. One of these latter three was the estate at Bradford which, as we have seen, was gifted by Æthelred II to the nuns of Shaftesbury about fifty years after Eadred's will as a refuge for both the nuns and the relics of his sainted brother.[41] However, even if it is indeed true that Bradford was a royal estate since the time of Aldhelm, it does not mean that it had to have continuously remained as such for the totality of the period up until the reign of Eadred. By the early tenth century many early *minsters*, having passed out of royal patronage prior to this point, had fallen back into royal hands for varying reasons including due to the effects of the Viking wars. Revealingly, the nearby abbey of Bath was given to the monks of Saint-Bertin by King Athelstan, in 944, in order to provide them with a refuge. This was despite its earlier existence as a *minster* church in its own right. This suggests that, by the mid tenth century, the crown had regained possession of the abbey and was able to give it away again. In this case, the reassertion of royal control over the Church estate at Bath seems to have occurred as early as the reign of Offa. This means that we can tentatively suggest that Bradford was a royal estate in the seventh century and it was definitely one by the reign of Eadred, even if ownership in the period between those two points cannot be confirmed either way.

The next time Bradford on Avon appears in the written record is in a document known as *Author B's* version of *Vita S. Dunstani* (*Life of St Dunstan*), as the meeting place of the royal assembly during the reign of Edgar, when Dunstan was made into a bishop in 957.[42] Edgar probably chose Bradford, as it was within a fairly fluid frontier zone between his kingdom of Mercia and his brother's kingdom of Wessex. Frontiers are liminal places and Dunstan as a man who had been abbot of Glastonbury, and would very soon become the bishop of Worcester, was a man who had connections both sides of the frontier and it should be expected that bishops from both Wessex and Mercia would have attended. It also seems a fitting place to have created a new bishop given the connection between Bradford and one of the most important early West Saxon bishops, the seventh-century Aldhelm. That Bradford was a significant royal estate probably further encouraged its selection as the venue for the council meeting.[43]

Whether Bradford was, or was not, continuously a royal estate after the time of Aldhelm, there does definitely seem to have been a church on the site prior to the charter of 1001, and the main evidence for this is in the form of sculpture found in the vicinity of the Late Saxon church of St Laurence (the 'Saxon Church'). There survives a cross fragment which was built into a wall of a house close to the church that contains animal art typical of the region and seems to be ninth century.[44] In addition, the stone sculpture now used in the altar has been most closely paralleled with manuscript art and in particular with the *Vespasian Psalter* (late eighth century) and the *Book of Kells* (late seventh century).[45] It may even be earlier than this, as the decoration compares well with the *millefiori*-work that appears on the early seventh-century Sutton Hoo (Suffolk) shoulder clasps.

This, albeit fragmentary, sculptural evidence points to the presence of a church in Bradford on Avon before the present 'Saxon Church', even if this church was not on exactly the same site. It has been suggested that these pre-existing features which included burial places – implied by cross-shaft fragments – would have affected the choice of the site of the later chapel.[46] However, while the existence of a church on the site was almost certainly influential in this decision, the significance of Bradford on Avon appears to have rested on more than just this. As has already been discussed, Bradford was a royal estate which had belonged to the West Saxon royal family since at least the time of Aldhelm, if a charter claiming to date from 705 and listing his monasteries as Malmesbury, Frome and Bradford on Avon is authentic.[47] Bradford was therefore not simply a conveniently located site but one which was truly fitting as the refuge for the relics of a royal prince due to its royal status and connection to that other prestigious royal West Saxon saint, Aldhelm. In addition, it was sited in the sensitive frontier zone of the Avon valley which had long associations with the expanding ambitions of the West Saxon royal house. As such, it had spiritual, historic and dynastic associations which resonated with the rulers of Wessex. This, in turn, suggests that a significant development was consciously being signalled by the granting of such an estate to Shaftesbury as the refuge for Edward's relics in 1001.

Bradford on Avon not only had a long history of royal and ecclesiastical connections but became the site of a very wealthy new church in the early eleventh century, which was sited at the centre of a productive estate; the latter status almost certainly well established by 1001. The lavish nature of the decoration of this new church and its architectural richness, including the sculptures known as the 'Bradford angels' which seem to date to a similar period to the church building, suggests that generous royal patronage was involved in its construction.

It has also been observed that the jointing of the stones at Bradford is remarkably fine and this would fit with the lavish quality of the decoration.[48] The chapel also seems to be 'more elaborate than others with seemingly similar status',[49] and bears a resemblance to the royal chapel at Cheddar.[50] If it is accepted that the church of St Laurence at Bradford was built in order to house the bones of Edward King and Martyr, then it should come as no surprise that it should compare with another royal chapel.

Bradford was not only a wealthy royal estate but also one which had previously been used as a refuge place well before the development of this role in 1001. As we saw in Chapter 5, a series of potential refuges for civilians and animals during periods of warfare have recently been identified, dating from the eighth or ninth century in the vicinity of the East Wansdyke. This suggests that Budbury, at Bradford on Avon, was one of these local refuge places.[51] As the stonework discussed earlier indicates, the *minster* church at Bradford was probably in existence by the early eighth century and was therefore a significant local church by the ninth century when this network of defensible places began to emerge in Wessex. At Bradford, as elsewhere, these were located at sites which combined an Iron Age hillfort, a royal estate and a *minster*. This may have had very ancient roots since, as we saw in Chapter 3, the alleged location of *Wirtgeornesburh* (Vortigern's fort) at Bradford on Avon suggests that it had been a defended place on the Avon frontier since the seventh century. All of this indicates that Æthelred was not just granting any estate to Shaftesbury, but rather one which had high prestige both as a royal estate and as a wealthy land-holding in its own right and, furthermore, was one which may well have had a role as a refuge in the past on the northern frontier of Wessex and, as such, was a fitting resting place and sanctuary for his brother's body.

What is particularly interesting about the likely site of the refuge place at Budbury is that excavation has revealed that its Iron Age defences were systematically razed at some point. This would have also removed any Anglo-Saxon additions to its defensive features. The nature of this destruction is striking. [52] What is intriguing is that this characteristic has been noted at a number of other sites, where Anglo-Saxon-period stone-wall defences were also razed, such as Daws Castle (Somerset), Cricklade (Wiltshire) and Christchurch (Dorset). A possible context for such destruction would be the reign of Cnut (1016-35); in which case the motivation would have been the removal of fortresses associated with his predecessor, Æthelred II, which could have continued to provide focal points for resistance to the new regime. [53]

At the time that Æthelred II granted Bradford to Shaftesbury, England was under increasing pressure from the new wave of Viking attacks. As a result,

Æthelred II and his leading counsellors sought heavenly assistance in their resistance to these attacks. This revealed itself in promoting the saintly cult of his murdered half-brother and in seeking the favour of heaven through the lavish gift of Bradford to the nuns at Shaftesbury. Even though the Avon valley was no longer a frontier zone it consequently found itself on a 'spiritual front line', as Æthelred II sought to defend his kingdom with every means at his disposal. This included the 1001 land grant to Shaftesbury and a law (known as V *Æthelred*), in 1008, which stipulated that a feast in honour of Edward King and Martyr should be celebrated throughout England. However, despite the strategies of Æthelred II, the Viking attacks continued to escalate and in 1016 this meant that the Avon valley once more emerged as a frontier between kings.

A Kingdom Frontier for the Last Time

In 1013, Svein of Denmark took command of the Viking forces invading England. Landing in the Humber estuary, the Northumbrians, parts of Lincolnshire, the Five Boroughs and the Danish settlers in the *Danelaw* accepted him as their king. Next, Svein moved south-westward and Oxford, Winchester and Bath surrendered to him. At Bath the western *thegns* submitted. This once again indicates the importance of Bath by the eleventh century. As well as being conveniently located at a point where the western Anglo-Saxon elites could meet with an invader who had secured control of the Midlands, it may have had additional symbolic value. It was, of course, the very place where Edgar had been crowned in 973; where better in the West Country for Svein to announce his newly won domination of England? The political echoes of that earlier ceremony undoubtedly enhanced Svein's claim to legitimacy; even though his was based on conquest rather than established right. Only London held out because Æthelred II was there. However, his position was now unsustainable and he fled into exile in Normandy. Svein of Denmark was now supreme in England.

However, in February, 1014 he died, and was succeeded by Cnut, his son. At this point in the complex proceedings the English elites switched sides. They sent messengers to Æthelred II, asking him to return. Cnut was forced to leave England. In 1015 the Vikings were back and, in April, Æthelred II died. His son, Edmund Ironside, succeeded to the kingdom but faced an exhausting series of battles against Cnut. These included battles fought in proximity to the Avon region at Penselwood (Somerset) and actually on the upper course of the 'Sherston Avon' at Sherston (Wiltshire). Regarding this battle, the later chronicler, John of Worcester, adds that this was 'in Hwicci', which is a curious reminder that the old kingdom of the Hwicce (long vanished) had not been entirely forgotten.[54] John of Worcester describes this battle as lasting two days, which is unlikely given other evidence suggesting that most contemporary battles were short, sharp affairs. He also adds the detail that an Anglo-Saxon nobleman, Earl Eadric Streona, attempted to panic the English by spreading the false news that Edmund Ironside had been killed on another part of the battlefield; an act of treachery all too likely to be true given this nobleman's track record of treason. John also recorded a tradition that Eadric defected to Cnut and took with him the units raised from Southampton and from Wiltshire. Despite the fierceness of the fighting, neither Edmund Ironside nor Cnut were able to secure victory and the result was a bloody draw. Years later a local legend would grow up around this battle and the unlikely figure of John Rattlebone, who staunched the blood flowing from a great wound in his abdomen with a slab of rock pressed against it, as he fought to the death alongside Edmund, his king. The legend is still preserved in the name of the well known public house – the Rattlebone Inn – at Sherston.

More inconclusive battles followed which wore down English resistance. Edmund Ironside – probably out of the necessity of trying to lessen the enemy forces ranged against him – was reconciled to Eadric Streona. Despite this, Eadric betrayed his king again; this time at the battle of Ashingdon (Essex) where English casualties were very high but once again the outcome was inconclusive. Eventually Edmund Ironside and Cnut met at Alney (Gloucestershire). With the war at stalemate they agreed to divide England. Edmund Ironside took Wessex and Cnut took Mercia.[55] Just a few months later, Edmund Ironside died. Cnut became ruler of the entire kingdom of England.

In 1016, at the Treaty of Alney, when Edmund Ironside and Cnut divided up the kingdom,[56] this once again briefly made the 'western Avon' a kingdom boundary. This was similar to the situation with Eadwig and Edgar in 957. This treaty saw the 'western Avon' form part of the boundary between the territory under Cnut's jurisdiction to the north and Edmund's to the south. However, due to the rapid death of Edmund Ironside following this treaty, England was once again united under the single kingship of Cnut. From this point onwards, the 'western Avon' was never again to be a kingdom boundary, although it would continue as a county and diocesan boundary due to its earlier position as a frontier between kingdoms.

Nevertheless, this same section of the 'western Avon' continued to be politically significant as it also featured as a boundary in Cnut's four-way division of the kingdom in 1017, since Cnut kept particular control of Wessex and – temporarily – Earl Eadric held Mercia; which would have been north of the Avon at this point in its course.[57] This same section of the Avon would therefore have also been the northern boundary of Earl Godwin's later earldom, west of Bath. Between Bath and the Severn it would have followed the same line of the river Avon as had the northern boundary of the earlier – and smaller – territory of Æthelweard '*Occidentalium Prouinciarum dux*' (*ealdorman* of the western shires), since this constituted western Wessex, whose northern border west of Bath followed the Avon. The reference to this earlier sub-division of the earldom of Wessex appears in a charter of 997.[58] Earl Godwin was a powerful nobleman, who rose to prominence during the reign of Cnut and his two sons, from 1016 to 1042. He continued to be highly – if controversially – influential during the reign of Edward the Confessor (1042–1066), who clearly resented being overshadowed by this over-mighty subject. Despite this, during the later years of the reign of Edward the Confessor, Godwin's son, Harold Godwinson, became even more influential than his father and in January 1066 succeeded Edward the Confessor as king of England. He would, of course, only hold the crown until October of that year when he was killed by the Normans at the battle of Hastings.

The Godwin family (as we briefly saw in Chapter 5) had a number of connections with the Avon valley. In 1051, following a serious rift with Edward the Confessor, Earl Godwin of Wessex and his sons were forced into exile. The *manuscript D* of the *Anglo-Saxon Chronicle* explains that it was from Bristol that his sons Harold, Leofwine and Swein left for exile in Ireland. This emphasises the well-established trading links between Bristol and Ireland. The *Chronicle* says that the ship was equipped and provisioned by Swein and we may surmise that Bristol was its home port. A military force was sent to prevent the escape, under the leadership of Bishop Aldred from London, but failed to do so. The same manuscript of the *Chronicle* adds that, at the mouth of the river Avon, bad weather nearly prevented the escape of the ship. In 1063, the same manuscript of the *Chronicle* – well informed with regard to Godwin-affairs – notes that Harold Godwinson (by this time earl of Wessex, following the death of his father) once again sailed from Bristol. This time, though, he was on official business, campaigning against the Welsh. Finally, in 1067 (and again in *manuscript D*), following Harold Godwinson's death at Hastings, his exiled sons landed at the mouth of the Avon and caused a great deal of destruction. Given that they were exiled by the new Norman rulers it is unclear what they hoped to achieve from this violent assault on fellow Anglo-Saxons. Whatever their aim, they failed in their attempt to seize control of Bristol due to the resistance of its citizens. Clearly, the Bristolians had no wish to provoke the anger of King William by siding with the disgruntled sons of the former king; perhaps especially so given the latter's rather vague but violent tactics. All of this emphasises both the importance of Bristol as a port, its dominance of the lower reaches of the Avon and its connections with Ireland. Clearly, the town had come a long way quickly since its development in the late tenth century. Interestingly, the later *Gesta Stephani* (*Life of Stephen*), written *c.* 1141, claimed that Bristol was a port capable of accommodating 'a thousand ships' and that the city 'seems to swim on the water'. This Anglo-Saxon port was – according to the later sixteenth-century writer, Leland, and other evidence – located in the area known as 'The Back' and today called 'Welsh Back'. From Bristol, Welsh and Anglo-Saxon slaves were shipped to Ireland in an early version of the city's slave trading role. It was a trade condemned after the Norman Conquest by Wulfstan (lived *c.* 1008–1095), the bishop of Worcester, whose diocese included Bristol (but not, of course, Bath due to the earlier tenth-century annexation by Edward the Elder). Such slaves may have been taken in warfare against the Welsh, as punishment for crimes or in conflicts within the state at times of political upheaval. For example, Earl Godwine enslaved some of the companions of the *ætheling* Alfred (Edward the Confessor's brother) in 1036 when Alfred returned from exile in Normandy; Earl Harold Godwinson took slaves when he landed in the West Country from Ireland in 1052 (according to *manuscript E* of the *Chronicle*), having previously been exiled; and supporters of Earl Morcar apparently seized 'many hundreds of people' in Northamptonshire as late as 1065 when they advanced south, having revolted against the rule of Earl Tosti in Northumbria.[59]

The Avon Valley at the End of Anglo-Saxon England

The accession of Cnut in 1016 finally ended the role of the river Avon as a kingdom frontier, although, as we have seen, it continued to be the boundary of one of the great earldoms of Anglo-Saxon England until this earldom was effectively abolished by the Norman, William the Conqueror, in 1071. However, even this was prone to fluctuations since earldoms were frequently sub-divided and different sub-sections temporarily bolted together. As a consequence, in 1045, Swein's earldom (in a sub-section of south-western Mercia) straddled the 'western Avon' since it also included Somerset and, in 1065, Harold Godwinson's earldom extended north of the Avon since it included south-western Mercia as well as most of historic Wessex.[60] Nevertheless, the Avon's past history continued to influence local government (shire) and Church boundaries and this had started much earlier, even while it was the boundary of much larger institutions of the state. To the west of Bath the old frontier had formed the shire (county) boundary between the shires of Somerset and Gloucestershire and the Church diocesan boundary between Wells (after 909 when it was formed out of the diocese of Sherborne) and Worcester. Bath is the anomaly and witnesses both of these boundaries looping north in order to encompass Bath within Somerset and the diocese of Wells, despite being north of the Avon. To the east of Bath the county boundary of Wiltshire and Gloucestershire and the diocesan boundary of Ramsbury (carved out of Winchester diocese in 909 and then in 1058 united with Sherborne) and Worcester, ignored the river

Avon and the old unity that straddled the Avon since the pre-Roman Dobunni continued to be asserted. This was a characteristic the Avon had maintained since the Late Iron Age. Earlier than 909 the respective boundaries with the diocese of Worcester would have been those of Sherborne and Winchester (the latter two dioceses being reorganised in 909). The similarity between the bishop of Worcester's diocese, as mapped in around 1291, and the areas of land that had earlier been granted within the kingdom of the Hwicce up to the year 821,[61] indicates that this diocesan boundary (and consequently the contiguous boundaries of dioceses that became shire boundaries for northern Somerset and north-western Wiltshire) was at least as old as 821 and almost certainly dated from long before the ninth century.

Shire (county) boundaries are somewhat conjectural before the eleventh century and even then were subject to alteration. It is generally assumed though that the shires of Wessex were in place (even if boundaries were not firmly fixed) before the ninth century. This is borne out by the first reference to the people of Wiltshire (in the form *Wilsætan*) dating from 800 and the more recognisable form *Wiltunscir* dating from 870;[62] the first mention of Somerset (in the form *Sumursætum*) dates from 845.[63] In both cases the Old English forms used indicate that what had originally been a term for a group of settlers eventually became a regional term. What is clear, though, is that the term already appears well established by the early ninth century. By way of contrast, Gloucestershire (in the form *Gleawcestrescir*) was not recorded before 1016,[64] and this shire was probably formed in the late tenth century by the amalgamation of earlier regional land units that had originally formed component parts of the kingdom of the Hwicce. Some of these earlier regional land units may have had sub-Roman or even Roman origins. These component parts included the 'Seven Hundreds of Cirencester', recorded in 1189, which may have had ancient origins in the sixth-century mini-kingdom of Cirencester that fell in 577; the 'Seven Hundreds of Grumbalds Ash' which features in a record of 1248 and which may originally have had Bristol as its administrative centre; Gloucester too may have been one of these original regional units but one some distance from the Avon valley, as was Winchcombe. Another such unit – and of direct relevance to this study – may have been centred on Bath but this, of course, had been annexed into Wessex and Somerset by the early tenth century. In each case they were also the sites of early *minsters*, which may once have been focal points of early tribal groups or mini-kingdoms.[65] By the eleventh century this system of shires converged on the Avon valley in the west and less so in the east.

The location of manors within particular shires in *Domesday Book* (1086) can be used to map the approximate course of these boundaries in Late Anglo-Saxon England. West of Bath, *Domesday Book* clearly shows Somerset to the south of the river and Gloucestershire to the north. This continued throughout the Middle Ages and into the modern period, with the exception of when the county of Avon, from 1974 to 1996, straddled the river. For these few years it constituted an administrative unit formed from parts of the historic counties of Gloucestershire and Somerset, together with the City of Bristol. When it ended, in 1996, the successor counties (the so-called 'unitary authorities' of Bath and North East Somerset, the City of Bristol, North Somerset, and South Gloucestershire) once more generally respected the historic role of the Avon as a boundary, with exceptions at Bath (an ancient anomaly) and Bristol (where administrative arrangements, which straddled the river to incorporate its southern suburbs, had existed for some time although the historic medieval city was sited on the northern bank, in Gloucestershire). What is clear is that in the twenty-first century the role of the river Avon as a civil local government boundary continues. The same applies to the northern course of the boundary of the diocese of Bath and Wells. In this, these boundaries basically fossilise a Late Anglo-Saxon arrangement which, as we have seen, itself fossilised a Late Iron Age one.

However, east of Bath the boundary between Wiltshire and Gloucestershire appears more interested in the *Fosse Way* as a frontier marker. This is both a modern and a medieval characteristic.[66] If there is any feature that seems to have influenced the course of Wiltshire's north-western border it is the Roman road. Even that, though, had only approximate influence since, at *Domesday Book* (1086), Thorngrove Hundred straddled it, Dunlow Hundred lay west of the road, as did part of Chedglow Hundred which lay between Ashley and Long Newnton (both now in Gloucestershire). However, in this last hundred there is a short correlation between the course of the county boundary and the Roman road west of Brokenborough and west of Kemble.[67] What this means is that the early medieval boundary paid less attention to the line of the *Fosse Way* than the modern one does. The modern county boundary, in contrast, follows the line of the Roman road from the vicinity of Three Shire Stones, north of Banner Down (which is north-east of Bath) to a point south-east of Marshfield (Gloucestershire); and then again from a point north-east of Easton Grey (Wiltshire), to the modern Kemble Airfield, just south-west of Jackaments Bottom, where the line of the Roman road meets the modern A433 (which then follows the line of the *Fosse Way* into Cirencester). However, at Kemble Airfield the modern county boundary turns sharply south-eastward, away from the line of the *Fosse Way*. Despite this, at least one could suggest that the Roman road was an 'influencing factor' in the older course of the boundary; even if less so than in the modern course. What is clear, though, is that the river Avon was not an influencing factor. In this too, as further west, the twenty-first century civil local government boundary generally fossilises a Late Anglo-Saxon arrangement which also fossilised a Late Iron Age one. On the 'eastern Avon', though, this boundary continuity determinedly ignores the river Avon, as it has done for two millennia. Continuity indeed on both halves of this 'river of two halves'!

CHAPTER 7

Making Sense of the Changing Evidence: 'a River of Two Halves'

This chapter draws together the evidence from over 1,000 years of history (from the Late Iron Age to the Norman Conquest) and identifies the key patterns that emerge from this analysis. It also explores the most likely reasons for that pattern, through the examination and assessment of the combination of historical, geographical and cultural influences that led to the contrasting use of the river Avon as a boundary west and east of Bath. To the west of Bath the river has been consistently used as a boundary since the Late Iron Age and that character is fossilised in the modern county and Church boundaries. To the east of Bath – with the exception of the period of the Viking Wars – the river failed to provide such a boundary and this continues to be the case. Clearly, the military, political and ecclesiastical use of the river as a frontier reveals it truly is a 'river of two halves.' That this ancient characteristic still influences its use in the twenty-first century is a remarkable example of historical continuity.

A Pattern in History

Throughout the period under study the river Avon was either a frontier, or a frontier region. However, it was a fluctuating one and one with differing degrees of importance at different points in time (e.g. kingdom, county, diocese) and the most striking feature of the Avon valley as a frontier, are the 'two stories' that it tells either side of the Limpley Stoke Valley.

West of the Limpley Stoke Valley, the Avon valley was consistently a boundary. In the pre-Roman period it appears to have defined an internal tribal boundary of the Dobunni as reflected in the distribution of the coins of Bodvoc and Corio/Catti. In the Roman period this area was (if Ptolemy is correct and his mention of both *Aquae Calidae* and the Mendips being in the territory of the Belgae suggests it was not a scribal error) separated off as a different administrative unit and given to the Belgae. In the sub-Roman period the Dobunni appear to have reoccupied Bath but the area south of the Avon transitioned into a separate political unit demarcated by West Wansdyke and culturally distinct pottery and settlement patterns. From the sixth century onwards, increasing Germanic pressure saw the Dobunnic kingdom north of the river re-emerge as the 'Anglo-Saxon' kingdom of the Hwicce, while south of the river it remained British until absorbed into Wessex. Following the absorption of the Hwicce into Mercia, the Avon became a boundary between two major kingdoms which was then followed by the shire and diocesan boundaries, until it ceased to be a kingdom boundary in the early tenth century with the demise of Mercia. The only exception to this pattern was Bath which, despite its geographical position north of the Avon, was annexed to political and ecclesiastical units to the south in the early tenth century.

East of the Limpley Stoke Valley the river has a more varied and fluctuating history; with a less definite characteristic as a frontier. It is almost as if this length of its course lacked a firm rooting as a boundary within regional traditional consciousness. The Avon east of Bath appears to have been straddled by the lands of the Dobunni, with pre-Roman Dobunnic culture stretching as far as the river Wylye and Salisbury Plain. This appears to have set the tone for the rest of the period with competing post-Roman kingdoms attempting to claim land either side of it; consequently, it became a *contested frontier zone* rather than a *distinct frontier based on the river itself*. As a result, both Wessex and Mercia contested influence at Malmesbury but, overall, each was pushing past the river, seeking a frontier line beyond it (in the case of Wessex, possibly based on the Roman road of the *Fosse Way* once the further Cotswolds were lost to Mercia). Temporary *Gewissaen* overlordship – from the direction of the Upper Thames – over the Hwicce until the 620s may have increased this sense that the 'eastern Avon' was not an acceptable political limit, which reinforced earlier arrangements and helped influence later developments. This may have been further reinforced by Winchester-based West Saxon perceptions that they had inherited the political sphere of influence of the Belgae; and that this included control of the Bath region. As a result, the kingdom frontier never settled on the 'eastern Avon' and no county or diocesan boundary followed the river east of the Limpley Stoke Valley. There is only one major exception, during the Viking Wars, when the river marked a military boundary between Wessex and the Danes along the entire length of its course.

A Pattern in the Landscape

The historic pattern is clear and it is that the use of the Avon as a frontier broadly divides at the Limpley Stoke Valley and this can be traced as far back as the Late Iron Age. The question is why? There are a number of possible reasons for this undeniable and consistent pattern of use (and non-use) of the river.

This pattern may have been prompted by distinct geographical features connected with the relief of the physical geography. The jumbled valleys around Bath, where the Cotswold hills dip to the river, certainly create a landscape quite unlike that found to west and east of this point. Approaching Bath from the east one encounters a striking combination of little valleys that causes the two 'halves' of the river Avon either side of this point to lack a sense of unity and cohesion. This seems in turn to have been reflected in political realities and so became self-reinforcing over time. If, at a local level, the river was perceived as being in two 'halves' then it should not come as a surprise to discover that these two halves have a different story to tell.

Areas of woodland on either bank at the Limpley Stoke Valley may have added to this sense of it being a dividing point. The presence of Selwood Forest (combined with additional woodland north of it) provided a significant barrier between the two regions east and west of this point. The distribution of Old English *gehæg* (wood-hedge) and *leah* (woodland/clearing) place names north and south of the Limpley Stoke Valley would suggest that this was a significantly wooded area.[1] Limpley Stoke itself contains the word *leah*. Not that this is to suggest that this constituted impenetrable wildwood. Nothing like that had existed in the area since the Neolithic (*c.* 4000 BC) and perhaps even further back into the Mesolithic. What it constituted was an area with a woodland coverage well above average and where clearances that had occurred by the Late Iron Age and Roman periods were replaced by secondary woodland regeneration in the sub- and post-Roman periods. It was the clearance of this secondary woodland that is reflected in the surviving place names.

Research into the pattern of minor place and field names on the eastern bank of the Avon, bordering the Limpley Stoke Valley corroborates the picture offered above. Old English (Anglo-Saxon) woodland names occur in large numbers in a concentrated geographical area. *Haga* or (*ge*)*hæg* survives in Haugh Farm and nearby Haugh Potticks Farm. 'Holt', probably a name for a single-species wood, survives in Holt. *Leah* survives in a great many minor names such as: Bradford Leigh, Frankleigh, Great Ashley and Little Ashley, Hartley, Leigh Grove Farm, Northleigh Farm, Warleigh, Winsley, and Woolley. Possibly relevant topographical field names (indicating probable occurrence of Old English, *leah*) appear on the 1842 Tithe Map. In Winsley Tithing these are: Great Stapeley (north-west of Winsley); Hemleaze (bordering Conkwell Wood); Longley (south-west of Haugh Farm) and the same area is the location of Longley Grove, Great Longley and Great Longley Wood; finally there is Norwood (north of Hartley). In Leigh and Woolley Tithing the field names include: Benleys (north-east of Woolley); Motleys (west of Bradford Leigh); and finally Tazley (west-south-west of Woolley).

These Old English words are very revealing. Whilst early Old English use of *leah* could refer to 'woodland', the most likely meaning in Wiltshire is 'clearing'. In this sense the word may refer to clearance of secondary, rather than primary, woodland. The word probably came into common usage with this meaning after 730.[2] It probably indicates either: the existence of old managed woodland which may have been so used in the Roman period or woodland/scrub which had regenerated in the post-Roman period and was then re-cleared for settlement or agricultural use. The plotting of Romano-British settlements underlying areas of later regenerated woodland in this area suggests the latter definition applies in these examples. Either way, *leah* is clearly indicative of woodland existing and recognised as ancient when English speakers arrived in any region;[3] and there have been suggestions, from examples found elsewhere, that *some* of this may have been primary – if well managed – forest and not regenerated from formerly cultivated areas.[4] The references to deer (in Hartley) and to wolves (in Woolley) may support the use of the term for 'wood', as well as for 'clearing'.

With regard to *haga* or *(ge)hæg*, the word means 'hedge' or 'enclosure' and its Wiltshire distribution is confined to the west and south-west of the county.[5] In close association with *leah*-names, as is the case in this area, it is indicative of ancient woodland surviving as field boundaries in the Anglo-Saxon period.

The place name and field name evidence clearly suggests that in the Anglo-Saxon period a crescent of woodland dominated the land to the north-east of the Limpley Stoke Valley. Even today the eastern side of the Avon valley from Bathford to Conkwell is still heavily wooded, as are both sides of the lower river Frome as it flows into the Avon. The western slopes, from Bathampton to Monkton Combe, are also still surprisingly wooded. It is clear that these are survivals of earlier, and even more extensive, woodland.

While this tract of woodland was not a large enough barrier to completely prevent the military expansion of the West Saxons it may have served to slow down penetration. As a result, it created two areas with different political characteristics and these proved tenacious. While the Avon to the west of Bath became a boundary to Mercian rulers pressing down from the Cotswolds, the Avon to the east was more likely to be absorbed into the emerging kingdom of Wessex rather than being used as a barrier between it and an earlier British kingdom and, from the seventh century, the Hwicce/Mercia. This situation may have been encouraged if the West Saxons considered themselves the inheritors of British political arrangements which had not considered the Avon to the east of Bath to be a frontier. The topographical and woodland 'barriers' that divided the land east and west of Bath were in no way impenetrable (indeed the area was relatively easily traversed) but the sense of differentness in people's minds appears to have been more potent. It is a reminder that a sense of local history and continuity is not to be underestimated, especially when correlated with traditional concepts of where 'legitimate boundaries' begin and end.

With regard to the north-western border of Wiltshire: as we saw in Chapter 6 this shows a closer (though imperfect) correlation between its course and the Roman road of the *Fosse Way*, rather than the course of the 'eastern Avon'. The county boundary in question and the route of the *Fosse Way* seem associated with the eastern edge of land above 61 metres and to the west of the *Fosse Way* the land higher than 122 m rises as a distinct landscape feature. This seems to have therefore generally informed the location of the county boundary when the river, further east, had been totally ignored.

The River Avon: a 'Story' of Remarkable Continuity

It is as if, while elites rise, fall and change, the local history was so engrained in the region that it dictated a response to the river fairly consistently over time. This may be a hint that many of the local elites did not change as often as they might appear to have done, from the apparent cultural and ethnic signals. There is, consequently, a remarkable degree of continuity in the two 'Avon stories', from the pre-Roman period to the eleventh century; and the origin of these contrasting 'stories' was rooted in the significant nature of the landscape in the vicinity of Bath and the Limpley Stoke Valley.

Notes

Chapter 1. The Main Evidence Base

1. See: Magennis, Swan, *A Companion to Ælfric* (2009), pp. 132–135.
2. Found in Whitelock , *English Historical Documents* (1979).
3. Whitelock, Douglas, Tucker, *The Anglo-Saxon Chronicle* (1961).
4. Garmonsway, *The Anglo-Saxon Chronicle (1972).*
5. A detailed examination of issues relating to the Anglo-Saxon Chronicle can be found in: Jorgensen, *Reading the Anglo-Saxon Chronicle: Language, Literature, History* (2010). Regarding how to understand and approach the different manuscripts, especially helpful is the chapter: Jorgensen, 'Introduction: Reading the Anglo-Saxon Chronicle', pp. 1–28 and especially Table 1, pp. 6–7.
6. http://www.kemble.asnc.cam.ac.uk/node/8.
7. For an online collection of Anglo-Saxon charters see: http://www. esawyer. org.uk/ browse/index.html.
8. For an overview see: Nash, *Coinage in the Celtic World* (1987); Hobbs, *British Iron Age Coins in the British Museum* (1996); Creighton, *Coins and Power in Late Iron Age Britain (2009).*
9. Gannon, *The Iconography of Early Anglo-Saxon Coinage* (2003), pp. 85–86.
10. Slotkin, 'The Fabula, Story and Text of Breuddwyd Rhonabwy' (1989), p. 98.

Chapter 2. From the Late Iron Age to Late Roman Britain: Order Imposed or Crisis Deferred?

1. Ekwall, *The Concise Oxford Dictionary of English Place names* (1960), p. 19.
2. Rivet, Smith, *The Place names of Roman Britain* (1979), p. 240.
3. Bede, *A History of the English Church and People* (1968).
4. *Ibid,* p. 56.

5.   *Ibid*, p. 68.
6.   *Ibid*, p. 104.
7.   Ekwall, *op. cit*, p. 453.
8.   Williamson, *Sutton Hoo and its Landscape* (2008), p. 140.
9.   Whitelock, Douglas, Tucker, *The Anglo-Saxon Chronicle* (1961), p. 11.
10. Myres, *The English Settlements* (1986), p. 136.
11. Whitelock, *English Historical Documents* (1979), p. 165.
12. *Ibid*, p. 171.
13. Lavelle, *Alfred's Wars* (2010), p. 326.
14. Bradbury, *The Routledge Companion to Medieval Warfare* (2004), p. 4.
15. Campbell, *The Anglo-Saxon State* (2000), p. 49.
16. http://finds.org.uk/ironagecoins/rulers.
17. The matter, though, is not without controversy. Recently an alternative interpretation has postulated that the original Roman place name was actually *Cironium*, not *Corinium*, and was derived from a river name meaning 'dark'. Coates, 'Rethinking Romano-British *Corinium*' (2013), pp. 81–91.
18. B. Walters, Director, Association of Roman Archaeology, 'Roman Wiltshire Day School', held at Bradford on Avon, April, 2013.
19. White, *Britannia Prima* (2007), p. 40.
20. M. Papworth, National Trust Regional Archaeologist (Wessex Region), personal comment, 2009. See: *Deconstructing the Durotriges*, Reading University: unpublished PhD thesis, (2007), later published as: Papworth, *Deconstructing the Durotriges*. (2008).
21. Laycock, *Britannia the Failed State* (2008), p. 34.
22. Webster, *The Roman Invasion of Britain* (2003), p. 60.
23. Leins, 'What can be Inferred from the Regional Stylistic Diversity of Iron Age coinage?', (2008), Map 5a.
24. *ibid*', Map 5b.
25. Todd, *Roman Britain* (1999), p. 37.
26. I. Leins, Curator of Iron Age and Roman Coins, Department of Coins and Medals, at the British Museum, personal comment, 2011.
27. Cunliffe, *Iron Age Communities in Britain* (2005), pp. 189–190; Laycock, *op cit, p.34*.
28. Papworth, *The Search for the Durotriges* (2011), p. 26.
29. Rivet, Smith, *op. cit*, p. 321.
30. *Ibid*, p. 492.
31. Jones, 'Cities and Urban Life' (2004), p. 163, Fig.10.1.
32. Yorke, *Wessex in the Early Middle Ages* (1995), p. 3.
33. Webster, *op. cit*, p.61; Papworth (2008), *op cit* and personal comment.
34. Cunliffe, op. cit, p. 190; C. Haselgrove, Professor of Archaeology, University of Leicester, personal comment, 2011.

35. Leins, personal comment, *op cit.*
36. Leins (2008), *op. cit*, Map 5b.
37. Rivet, Smith, *op. cit*, pp. 255–6.
38. *Ibid*, p.144.
39. Mattingly, *An Imperial Possession* (2006), p. 399.
40. White, *op. cit*, p. 40.
41. Salway, *Roman Britain* (1981), Map VII.
42. White, *op. cit*, p. 39 and p. 41.
43. Laycock (2008), *op cit*, p. 34.
44. Laycock, *Warlords* (2009a), p. 54, pp. 59–60, pp. 91–3.
45. Laycock (2008), *op. cit*, pp. 140–1.
46. Costen, *The Origins of Somerset* (1992), p. 53, surveys the evidence for Keynsham, Brislingon, Combe Down and Wellow I, concluding that alongside the evidence for destruction must be set the evidence for continued occupation, or reoccupation, that lasted until near the end of the fourth century. Clearly, the evidence is complex and capable of supporting more than one interpretation.

Chapter 3. From Imperial Province to 'Failed State': Wars, Boundaries and Disintegration

1.   Zosimus, *New History*, Book VI, Chapters 5–6.
2.   *Ibid*, Book VI, Chapter 10.
3.   Esmonde Cleary, 'The Roman to Medieval Transition' (2001).
4.   Halsall, *Worlds of Arthur* (2013), p. 246.
5.   Jones, *The End of Roman Britain* (1996).
6.   *Ibid*, p. 250.
7.   Whittock, *A Brief History of Life in the Middle Ages* (2009), pp. 105–6.
8.   Gerard, 'The End of Roman Bath' (2008), pp. 24–31.
9.   Costen, *Anglo-Saxon Somerset* (2011), pp. 17–19.
10. Campbell, Bowles, 'Byzantine Trade to the Edge of the World' (2009), p. 309, Fig. 20.5.
11. Rahtz, *'The Dobunnic Area in post-Roman times'*, (2003), p. 27.
12. *Ibid*, p. 27.
13. Reynolds, 'The Early Medieval Period', (2006), pp. 133–160.
14. Dark, *Civitas to Kingdom* (1994), pp. 123–4.
15. Dixon, 'Thirty-five Years at Crickley' (2005), p. 394
16. Rahtz, *op. cit*, p. 25.
17. *Ibid*, p. 25.
18. Costen, *op. cit*, p. 18.
19. Campbell, Bowles, *op. cit*, p. 301.
20. White, *Britannia Prima* (2007), *p. 204.*

21. Sims-Williams, 'The Settlement of England in Bede and the Chronicle', (2007), pp. 33–34. For a more sympathetic, if cautious, interpretation see: *Harrison, The Framework of Anglo-Saxon History* (2010), p. 133. And for a more confident assertion of a pre-seventh-century date for the recording of Farinmail's name see: Charles-Edwards, *Wales and the Britons* (2012), p. 381 and note 2.
22. White, *op. cit*, p. 204.
23. De La Bedoyere, *Roman Britain: A New History* (2010), p. 260.
24. *Ibid,* p. 266.
25. *Ibid,* p. 267.
26. Bowles, *Rebuilding the Britons (2007), p. 452.*
27. Ó Floinn, 'Patrons and Politics' (2001), pp. 6–7.
28. White, *op. cit*, p. 199.
29. *Ibid,* p. 199.
30. *Ibid.*
31. Gardner, 'The Wansdyke Dikat?' (1998). See also: Gardner, 'The Land of Cyngar the Priest' (2009), pp. 42–52.
32. Reynolds, Langlands, 'Social Identities on the Macro Scale a Maximum View of Wansdyke' (2007), p. 16. See also: Whittock, 'Reflections on the cultural context and function of the West Wansdyke' (1988), pp. 2–5.
33. Reynolds, *op. cit*, p. 140.
34. Reynolds, Langlands, *op. cit, pp. 35–6.*
35. Erskine, 'The West Wansdyke' (2007), pp. 102–3.
36. Yorke, *Wessex in the Early Middle Ages* (1995), p. 22.
37. Reynolds, Langlands, *op. cit*, p. 34.
38. Erskine, *op. cit*, p. 95.
39. *Ibid,* p. 102.
40. *Ibid,* p. 103.
41. Laycock, *Britannia the Failed State* (2008), p. 145.
42. *Ibid, p. 198.*
43. Harvey, 'Shaftesbury Abbey's 12th century Rentals for Bradford on Avon' (1998), p. 79.
44. Grundy, 'The Ancient Woodland of Wiltshire' (1939), pp. 576–9.
45. Charter S 899, in Kelly, *Charters of Shaftesbury Abbey* (1996), p. 116.
46. Fowler, 'Wansdyke in the Woods' (2001), pp. 179–198.
47. Laycock, Warlords (2009a), p. 54.
48. Laycock (2008), *op. cit*, p. 146. See also: Laycock, 'Buckles and Bosnia. Britannia, the Threat Within' (2006), pp. 10–15.
49. Laycock (2008), *op cit*, pp. 164–5.
50. Cunliffe, 'Locating the Dobunni', (2003), p. 15.
51. White, *op. cit*, p. 175.

52. *Ibid*, p. 202.
53. Laycock, 'Buckles, Belts and Borders' (2009b), pp. 12–19.
54. *Ibid*, p. 234.
55. Whitelock *English Historical Documents* (1979), p. 157.
56. Yorke, *Kings and Kingdoms of Early Anglo-Saxon England* (1990), p. 135.
57. Costen, *op. cit,* p. 15.
58. Wickham, *Framing the Early Middle Ages* (2005), p. 345.
59. Yorke (1990), *op. cit,* p. 136.
60. Whitelock, *op. cit,* pp. 156–165.
61. Yorke (1995), *op. cit, p.* 57.
62. The year 665 has been suggested. See: http://www.fordham.edu/halsall/source/ annalescambriae.asp.
63. Geoffrey of Monmouth, *The History of the Kings of Britain* (1966), p. 217.
64. Slotkin, 'The Fabula, Story and Text of Breuddwyd Rhonabwy' (1989), p. 98.
65. Halsall, *op. cit,* pp. 256–7.
66. Bede, *A History of the English Church and People* (1968), I.16, p. 58.
67. William of Malmesbury, *Gesta Regum Anglorum* (1998), i.19.2, p. 43.
68. Whitelock, *op cit*, p. 165.

Chapter 4. Wars in the West: a Boundary of Anglo-Saxon Kingdoms
        NOTE: charters are identified by their 'Sawyer number'. 'Sawyer numbers' act as a common reference system for Anglo-Saxon charters. So, S 148 (796) gives the charter by its 'Sawyer number' and its date. These can be accessed, and the details of these charters examined at: http://www.esawyer.org.uk/browse/sawno.html.
1. Whitelock, *English Historical Documents* (1979), pp. 156–7.
2. *Ibid*, p. 158.
3. Koch, *Celtic Culture* (2006), p. 393.
4. Bede *A History of the English Church and People* (1968), I.16, p. 232.
5. William of Malmesbury, *Gesta Regum Anglorum* (1998), i.19.2, p. 43.
6. Ashley, 'The lay intellectual in Anglo-Saxon England' (2008), p. 230, p. 232 and pp. 235–6 for exploration of Æthelweard's 'agenda'.
7. Aston, Isles, *The Archaeology of Avon* (1984), p. 77.
8. White, *Britannia Prima* (2007), p. 204.
9. In compiling this overview we were greatly assisted by the information recorded in the *Bath and North East Somerset Council Monument List Report* provided by Rod Millard; the online information available for Wiltshire on the *Wiltshire and Swindon Sites and Monument Record* at http://history.wiltshire.gov.uk/smr/ smr_search.php; the information on

the *Historical Environment Record* for South Gloucestershire provided by Paul Driscoll; the information on the *Historical Environment Record* for Bristol provided by Peter Insole.

10. Reynolds, 'The Early Medieval Period' (2006), p. 141.
11. Symonds, 'Corinium's Dead' (2013), p. 34.
12. Aston, Isles, *op cit*, p. 79.
13. SMR Number: MBN2042, Bath and North-East Somerset Council.
14. Eagles, 'Anglo-Saxon Presence and Culture in Wiltshire' (2001), p. 201.
15. *Current Archaeology, May, 2013, Issue 278, p. 8.*
16. Yorkston, *Archaeological Evaluation at Rodway Hill Sports ground Pomphrey Hill Road, Mangotsfield* (2008). For the *minster at Bitton see the South Gloucestershire HER, PRN 10348.*
17. S 148 (769).
18. Williams, *Kingship and Government in Pre-Conquest England* (1999), p. 16.
19. See: Kelly, *Charters of Bath and Wells* (2007), p. 3; S 51 (675).
20. Sims-Williams, *Religion and Literature in Western England* (1990), p. 31.
21. Edwards, *Charters of the Early West Saxon Kingdom* (1988), p. 222.
22. Kelly (2007) *op cit*, p. 3.
23. *Ibid*, p. 62.
24. Bede, *Ecclesiastical History of the English People* (1990), IV.23, p. 245.
25. Sims-Williams, *op. cit*, p. 34; charters S 1165 (672/674) and S 70 (671).
26. Stenton, *Anglo-Saxon England* (1943), pp. 45–6; John, *Reassessing Anglo-Saxon England* (1996), p. 53.
27. A point well made by Dumville, 'The Terminology of Overkingship in Early Anglo-Saxon England' (1997), p. 346.
28. S 207 (855).
29. Edwards, op. cit, pp. 220–1.
30. S 1257 (781). See also: Hooke, *The Anglo-Saxon Landscape* (1985), p. 15 and p. 76.
31. Kelly (2007), op. cit, pp. 6–7.
32. William of Malmesbury, *The Deeds of the Bishops of England* (2002), p. 213; and Matthew Paris, *Chronica Majora (1872–83), i, p. 356.*
33. Williams, *op. cit*, p. 27; S 265 (757/8).
34. *Ibid*, p. 27.
35. *Ibid*, pp. 27–8.
36. S 148 (796). See also S 149 (796), Kelly (2007), *op. cit, pp. 7–8.*
37. Lapidge, Blair, Keynes, *The Blackwell Encyclopaedia of Anglo-Saxon England* (1999), p. 54.

38. Kemble, *Codex Diplomaticus Aevi Saxonici* (1839-48), no.590; S 210 (864).
39. Eagles, *op. cit*, p. 223.
40. Hooke, *op. cit*, p.16.
41. Haslam, *Anglo-Saxon Towns in Southern England* (1984), p. 115.
42. S 1166 (680).
43. S 71 (680/1) and S 73 (681).
44. S 1169 (685).
45. S 231 (682) and S 234 (688).
46. S 1170 (688).
47. S 1245 (675).
48. William of Malmesbury, *Gesta Pontificvm Anglorvm* (2007), pp. 530–531.
49. Kirby, *The Earliest English Kings* (2000), p. 98.
50. *S 1170 (688)*.
51. Aldhelm *Aldhelmi et ad Aldhelmum epistulae* (1919), Ep.10 (13); Lapidge, Herren, *Aldhelm: The Prose Works* (1979).
52. Williams, *op. cit*, p. 23 and p. 53. Also: Kelly, *Charters of Malmesbury Abbey, Anglo-Saxon (*2005), pp. 147–150 for the identification of the location of the estate granted to Malmesbury by Baldred.
53. Williams, *op. cit*, p. 27.
54. Yorke, *Wessex in the Early Middle Ages (1995), p. 61.*
55. S 265 (757/8).
56. S 260 (758).
57. S 149 (796).
58. S 320 (838/9), S 294a, S 294b (844), S 301 (850), S 305 (854), S 306 (854), S 356 (871).
59. S 210 (864).
60. S 146 (796).
61. S 1187 (804).
62. Hare, 'Anglo-Saxon Berkeley' (2013), p. 121.
63. http://www.buildinghistory.org/bristol/origins.shtml.
64. South Gloucestershire HER, PRN 10348.
65. S 889 (1001).
66. See: English Heritage (http://www.pastscape.org/default.aspx) Cowage Farm, Norton. MONUMENT NO. 1200155.
67. Hill, *An Atlas of Anglo-Saxon England* (1981), p. 101 and p. 106.

Chapter 5. War Zone: the Avon Valley in the Viking Wars

1. Ekwall, *The Concise Oxford Dictionary of English Place names* (1960), p. 441, p. 181, p. 307.
2. *Asser, Life of King Alfred* (1983), 9, p. 69.

3. Campbell, *Chronicon Æthelweardi* (1962), p. 38.

4. Whittock, H., The Avon Valley as a Frontier Region, From the Fourth to the Eleventh Century (unpublished dissertation in the department of Anglo-Saxon, Norse and Celtic, Cambridge University, 2010), p. 22.

5. SMR Number: MBN1216, Bath and North-East Somerset Council.

6. Whitelock, *English Historical Documents* (1979), p. 195.

7. Campbell, *op. cit*, p. 42.

8. Asser, *op. cit*, 52, p. 83.

9. Haslam, *Anglo-Saxon Towns in Southern England* (1984), pp. 132–6

10. Campbell, *op. cit*, p. 43.

11. Asser, *op. cit*, 56, p.84.

12. Aston, Isles, *The Archaeology of Avon* (1984), p. 85.

13. S 692 (961), quoted in: Grundy, *The Saxon Charters and Field Names of Somerset* (1935), pp. 179–81.

14. S 711 (963), *ibid*, pp. 190–2.

15. S 735 (965), *ibid*, pp. 193–5.

16. S 414 (931), *ibid*, pp. 182–4.

17. S 431 (936), *ibid*, pp. 186–189.

18. Haslam, *op. cit*, p. 115

19. *Ibid*, p. 111.

20. *Ibid*, p. 112.

21. S 629 (956).

22. Leech, 'The medieval defences of Bristol revisited' (1997), pp. 18–19.

23. Ford, Brady, Teague, *From Bridgehead to Brewery* (2012), Chapter 2, 'The Natural Landscape and Early Development to *c.* 1225', p. 3. We are grateful to Peter Insole, Archaeological Officer Bristol City Council, for allowing us to consult this unpublished report.

24. Ford, *Brady, Teague, op. cit*, Chapter 5, 'Discussion', p. 2.

25. Boore, *Excavations at Tower Lane Bristol* (1984), p. 11.

26. Grinsell, *The History and Coinage of the Bristol Mint* (1986), p. 25.

27. For more on Cnut's minting of coins at Bristol see: *Grinsell, The Bristol Mint* (1972), p. 24; Dolley, Metcalf, 'Cnut's Quatrefoil Type in English Cabinets of the Eighteenth Century' (1958), p. 71.

28. Ponsford, *Bristol Castle* (1979), vol.1, pp. 23–27.

29. Leech, *op. cit*.

30. http://www.buildinghistory.org/bristol/origins.shtml.

31. Whitelock, *op. cit*, p. 212

32. Campbell, *op cit*, p. 52.

33. Keynes, Lapidge, *Alfred the Great* (1983), p. 224.

34. Kirby, *The Earliest English Kings* (2000), p. 176

35. Whitelock, *op. cit*, p. 209.

36. Haslam, 'King Alfred and the Vikings' (2005), p. 130, p. 131, p. 132, p. 143.

37. Whittock, 'The Annexation of Bath by Wessex', (2012), pp. 46–53.

38. Edward the Elder, Bath penny, mint-name '*BAÐ*' and title '*REX SAXONVM*', 1.81 g. BMC 1, ex Cuerdale hoard, British Museum.

39. Lyon, 'The coinage of Edward the Elder', (2001), p. 74.

40. Grierson, Blackburn, *Medieval European Coinage* (1986), p. 314.

41. Edward the Elder, Bath penny, mint-name '*BA*' and title '*REX SAXONVM*', 1.61 g. Fitzwilliam Museum, CM.1.353-1990, ex C. E. Blunt collection, Fitzwilliam Museum, Cambridge.

42. Personal comment by G. Williams, Curator of Early Medieval Coinage, British Museum, 2009.

43. O'Leary, 'Excavations at Upper Borough Walls, Bath' (1981), p. 1.

44. These were: Chichester, Exeter, Portchester and Winchester. See: Schoenfeld, 'Anglo-Saxon Burhs and Continental Burgen' (1994), p. 59.

45. Abels, Morillo, 'A Lying Legacy?' (2005), p. 8.

46. Barber, Halsey, Lewcun, Philpotts, *Excavations at South Gate, Bath, 2007–8*, (forthcoming).

47. Blair, *The Church in Anglo-Saxon Society* (2005), p. 333.

48. SMR Number: MBN1927, Bath and North-East Somerset Council.

49. SMR Number: MBN1929, Bath and North-East Somerset Council.

50. SMR Number: MBN4905, Bath and North-East Somerset Council.

51. British Museum, 18546-21.28.

52. British Museum, Grueber 137. For a comparison of these coins with the Bath issue of Edward the Elder see: North, *English Hammered Coinage* (1994) p. 35.

53. *Ibid*, pp. 125–126.

54. *Ibid*, pp. 126–129.

55. *Ibid*, pp. 119–120.

56. Brooks, 'Henry Loyn Memorial Lecture' (2003), p. 47.

57. Grierson, Blackburn, *op. cit*, p. 314.

58. North, *op. cit, p.* 126.

59. Thorn, Thorn, *Domesday Book: Wiltshire* (1979), B.4; Williams, Martin, *Domesday Book: a Complete Translation* (2003), p. 162.

60. See Round, 'The third penny' (1919), pp. 62–64.

61. Baker, Brookes, 'From Frontier to Border' (2011), p. 111.

Chapter 6. A Fluctuating Frontier in an Increasingly United England

1. Foot, *Æthelstan* (2011), p. 17.

2. Whitelock, *English Historical Documents* (1979), p. 218.

3. Interestingly, Athelstan's cousins who were killed at the battle – Ælfwine and Æthelwine – were also buried at Malmesbury. This is also found in William of Malmesbury, is a credible claim given Athelstan's later

burial there and does illustrate the close relationship between Athelstan and Malmesbury.

4. See: Whittock, 'Why does the north-western boundary of Wiltshire ignore the river Avon?' (2012), pp. 96–104.
5. S 454 (939).
6. S 415 (931).
7. S 434 (937).
8. S 435 (937).
9. S 436 (937).
10. S 414 (931).
11. S 476 (941).
12. S 508 (946).
13. Florence of Worcester, *Chronicon ex Chronicis*, (1848-9), I, p. 137.
14. S 610 (956).
15. S 643 (957).
16. Kelly *Charters of Bath and Wells* (2007), p. 13.
17. S 627 (956).
18. S 661 (956).
19. S 664 (959). The earlier grant was S 414, of 931.
20. Kelly (2007), *op. cit*, p. 14 and Kelly, *Charters of Malmesbury Abbey* (2005), p. 23.
21. Kelly (2005), *op. cit*, p. 23.
22. S 629 (956).
23. S 1577.
24. Gretsch, *The Intellectual Foundations of the English Benedictine Reform* (1999), p. 306.
25. According to John of Worcester and William of Malmesbury.
26. Alexander, *The Earliest English Poems* (1977), pp. 28–29.
27. Marsden, *The Cambridge Old English Reader* (2004), p. 323.
28. Lambdin, Lambdin, *Encyclopedia of Medieval Literature* (2013), p. 444.
29. Karkov, *The Ruler Portraits of Anglo-Saxon England* (2004), p. 104.
30. Thormann, 'The Anglo-Saxon Chronicle Poems' (1997), p. 70.
31. Karkov, *op cit*, p. 104.
32. Clarke, *Writing Power in Anglo-Saxon England* (2012), p. 73.
33. Lavelle, *Aethelred II* (2002), p. 30.
34. Ekwall, *The Concise Oxford Dictionary of English Place names* (1960), p. 4.
35. SMR Number: MBN2445, Bath and North-East Somerset Council.
36. SMR Number: MBN8266, *ibid*.
37. S 405 (930), S 422 & S 433 (933).
38. S 473 (940).

39. S 1445 (924).
40. S 1515 (955).
41. S 899 (1001).
42. There has been debate as to whether this record really refers to Bradford on Avon. The cause of this confusion is partly due to the variant spellings of the assembly site. *Author B*'s version of the *Vita S. Dunstani* is preserved in three different manuscripts (*manuscripts A, C, D*) which were all written during the late tenth or early eleventh century. The meeting place is named as *Bradanford* in *manuscripts A* and *C*, but as *Brandanford* in *manuscript D*. Corroborative evidence for the spelling found in *manuscripts A* and *C* is found in the spelling *Bradford* in William of Malmesbury's account of this royal assembly. However, there are nine places in England named Bradford: Bradford (Cornwall), Bradford (Derbyshire), Bradford (Devon), Bradford Abbas (Dorset), Bradford Peverell (Dorset), Bradford (Lancashire), Bradford on Tone (Somerset), Bradford on Avon (Wiltshire) and Bradford (Yorkshire). Of these, though, the only one sited on the border of Wessex and Mercia – and therefore a candidate for the meeting in question – is Bradford on Avon.
43. Hinton, 'Recent Work at the Chapel of St Laurence, Bradford on Avon, Wiltshire', (2009), p. 195.
44. Plunkett, 'Mercian and West Saxon Decorative Stone-Sculpture' (1984), p. 383.
45. Allen, Anderson, *The Early Christian Monuments of Scotland* (1993), pp. 291–2.
46. Hinton, *op. cit*, p. 195; Cramp, *South West England, Corpus of Anglo-Saxon Stone Sculpture 7 (2006), pp. 202–3.*
47. S 1251a (705).
48. Brown, *The Arts in Anglo-Saxon England* (1925), p. 298.
49. Hinton, *op. cit*, p. 207.
50. Rahtz, *The Saxon and Medieval Palaces at Cheddar* (1979), pp. 192–233.
51. Baker, Brookes, 'From Frontier to Border' (2011), p. 111.
52. Roy Canham, personal comment.
53. Haslam, 'Daws Castle, Somerset, and civil defence measures in southern and midland England in the ninth to eleventh centuries' (2011), pp. 196–227, and personal comment.
54. Whitelock, *op. cit*, p. 249, note 7.
55. *Anglo-Saxon Chronicle, manuscript E.*
56. Hill, *An Atlas of Anglo-Saxon England* (1981), p. 71.
57. *Anglo-Saxon Chronicle, manuscripts A* and *E.*
58. S 891 (997).

59. *Regia Anglorum.* http://www.regia.org/earner.htm. For the *Chronicle* references to the events of 1052 and 1065 see: Whitelock, Douglas, Tucker, *The Anglo-Saxon Chronicle* (1961), p. 124 and p. 138.

60. Hill, *op. cit*, p. 105.

61. Bassett, 'In Search of the Origins of Anglo-Saxon Kingdoms' (1989), p. 9, Fig.1.2.

62. Ekwall, *op. cit*, p. 521.

63. *Ibid,* p. 430.

64. *Ibid,* p. 199.

65. Hooke, *The Anglo-Saxon Landscape (1985), pp. 75–76, p. 91.*

66. See: Whittock, *op cit.*

67. Thorn, Thorn, *Domesday Book: Wiltshire* (1979), map of Wiltshire Northern Hundreds.

Chapter 7. Making Sense of the Changing Evidence: 'A River of Two Halves'

1. Gover, Mawer, Stenton, *The Place names of Wiltshire* (1939), appendices, map of distribution of *leah* and *(ge)hæg names.*

2. Gelling, *Place names in the Landscape* (1984), p. 198.

3. *Ibid,* p. 199.

4. Rackham, *Trees and Woodland in the British Landscape* (1976), p. 56.

5. Gover, Mawer, Stenton, *op. cit*, p. 416.

Bibliography

Abels R., S. Morillo, 'A Lying Legacy? A Preliminary Discussion of Images of Antiquity and Altered Reality in Medieval Military History', *Journal of Medieval Military History* III (2005), pp. 1-13.

Aldhelm, *Aldhelmi et ad Aldhelmum epistulae*, R. Ehwald, (ed.), (Berlin: MGH, 1919).

Alexander, M. (transl.), *The Earliest English Poems* (Harlow: Penguin, 1977).

Allen, J. R., J. Anderson (eds.), *The Early Christian Monuments of Scotland* (Edinburgh, 1903, reprinted Balgavies: Pink Foot Press, 1993).

Ashley, S., 'The lay intellectual in Anglo-Saxon England: Æthelweard and the politics of history', in P. Wormald, L. Nelson, *Lay Intellectuals in the Carolingian World* (Cambridge: Cambridge University Press, 2008), pp. 218–245.

Asser, *Life of King Alfred*, in S. Keynes, M. Lapidge (transl.), *Alfred the Great. Asser's Life of King Alfred and other contemporary Sources* (Harmondsworth: Penguin, 1983), pp. 66–110.

Aston, M., R. Isles, *The Archaeology of Avon* (Bristol: Avon County Council, 1984).

Baker, J., S. Brookes, 'From Frontier to Border: The Evolution of Northern West Saxon Territorial Delineation in the Ninth and Tenth Centuries', *Anglo-Saxon Studies in Archaeology and History*, 17 (2011), pp. 108–123.

Barber, B., C. Halsey, M. Lewcun, C. Philpotts, *Excavations at South Gate, Bath, 2007 –8, MOLA Monograph Series* (London: Museum of London, forthcoming).

Bassett, S., 'In Search of the Origins of Anglo-Saxon Kingdoms', in S. Bassett (ed.), *The Origins of Anglo-Saxon Kingdoms* (London: Leicester University Press, 1989), pp. 3–27.

Bede, *A History of the English Church and People*, L. Sherley-Price (transl.), (Harlow: Penguin, 1968).

Bede, *Ecclesiastical History of the English People*, L. Sherley-Price (transl.) and D. H. Farmer (ed.), (Harlow: Penguin, 1990).

Blair, J., *The Church in Anglo-Saxon Society* (Oxford: Oxford University Press, 2005).

Boore, E. J., *Excavations at Tower Lane Bristol* (Bristol: City of Bristol Museum and Art Gallery, 1984).

Bowles, C. , *Rebuilding the Britons: The Postcolonial Archaeology of Culture and Identity in the Late Antique Bristol Channel Region* (Oxford: BAR, British Series, 2007).

Bradbury, J., *The Routledge Companion to Medieval Warfare* (Abingdon: Routledge, 2004).

Brooks, N., 'Henry Loyn Memorial Lecture: English identity from Bede to the Millennium', *The Haskins Society Journal*, 14 (2003), pp. 35–51.

Brown, B., *The Arts in Anglo-Saxon England: Anglo-Saxon Architecture II* (London: John Murray, 1925).

Campbell, A. (ed. and transl.), *Chronicon Æthelweardi: The Chronicle of Athelweard* (London, Edinburgh: Thomas Nelson, 1962).

Campbell, E., C. Bowles, 'Byzantine Trade to the Edge of the World: Mediterranean Pottery Imports to Atlantic Britain in the 6th Century', in M. Mundell Mango (ed.), *Byzantine Trade, 4th–12th Centuries: the Archaeology of Local, Regional and International Exchange* (Farnham: Ashgate Publishing, 2009), pp. 297–314 .

Campbell, J., *The Anglo-Saxon State* (London: Hambledon, 2000).

Charles-Edwards, T. M., *Wales and the Britons, 350-1064* (Oxford: Oxford University Press, 2012).

Clarke, C., *Writing Power in Anglo-Saxon England: Texts, Hierarchies, Economies* (Cambridge: D. S. Brewer, 2012).

Coates, R., 'Rethinking Romano-British *Corinium*', *The Antiquaries Journal*, volume 93 (2013), pp. 81–91.

Costen, M., *The Origins of Somerset* (Manchester: Manchester University Press, 1992).

Costen, M., *Anglo-Saxon Somerset* (Oxford: Oxbow Books, 2011).

Cramp, R., *South West England, Corpus of Anglo-Saxon Stone Sculpture 7* (Oxford: Oxford University Press, 2006).

Creighton, J., *Coins and Power in Late Iron Age Britain* (Cambridge: Cambridge University Press, 2009).

Cunliffe, B., 'Locating the Dobunni', in M. Ecclestone, N. Holbrook, A. Smith (eds.), *The Land of the Dobunni: a Series of Papers Relating to the Transformation of the Pagan, Pre-Roman, Tribal Lands into Christian, Anglo-Saxon Gloucestershire and Somerset* (Great Dunham: Heritage Marketing and Publications Ltd, 2003), pp. 12–16.

Cunliffe, B., *Iron Age Communities in Britain: An Account of England, Scotland and Wales from the Seventh Century BC until the Roman Conquest* (Abingdon: Routledge, 2005).

Dark, K. R., *Civitas to Kingdom: British Political Continuity 300-800* (London: Leicester University Press, 1994).

De La Bedoyere, G., *Roman Britain: A New History* (London: Thames and Hudson, 2010).

Dixon, P., 'Thirty-five Years at Crickley', *Current Archaeology*, 200 (2005), pp. 390–395.

Dolley, R. H. M., D. M. Metcalf, 'Cnut's Quatrefoil Type in English Cabinets of the Eighteenth Century', *British Numismatic Journal*, 29 (1958), pp. 69–81.

Dumville, D. N., 'The Terminology of Overkingship in Early Anglo-Saxon England', in J. Hines (ed.), *The Anglo-Saxons: From the Migration Period to the Eighth Century* (Woodbridge: Boydell Press, 1997), pp. 345–373.

Eagles, B., 'Anglo-Saxon Presence and Culture in Wiltshire *c.* 450-675', in P. Ellis (ed.), *Roman Wiltshire and After: Papers in Honour of Ken Annable* (Devizes: Wilshire Archaeological and Natural History Society, 2001), pp. 199–233.

Edwards, H., *Charters of the Early West Saxon Kingdom* (Oxford: BAR, British Series, 1988).

Ekwall, E., *The Concise Oxford Dictionary of English Place-names* (4th edn., Oxford: Oxford University Press, 1960).

Erskine, J., 'The West Wansdyke: an Appraisal of the Dating, Dimensions and Construction Techniques in the Light of Excavated Evidence', *The Archaeological Journal*, 164 (2007), pp. 80–108.

Esmonde Cleary, S., 'The Roman to Medieval Transition', in S. James, M. Millett, *Britons and Romans: Advancing an Archaeological Agenda* (York: CBA Research Report 125, 2001), pp 90–97.

Florence of Worcester, *Chronicon ex Chronicis*, B. Thorpe (ed.), 2 vols, (London: English Historical Society, 1848-9).

Foot, S., *Æthelstan: The First King of England* (New Haven and London: Yale University Press, 2011).

Ford, B. M., K. Brady, S. Teague, *From Bridgehead to Brewery: Finzels Reach Bristol, Draft for Reference Text* (Oxford: Oxford Archaeology South, April 2012).

Fowler, P., 'Wansdyke in the Woods: An Unfinished Roman Military Earthwork for a Non-event', in P. Ellis (ed.), *Roman Wiltshire and After: Papers in Honour of Ken Annable* (Devizes: Wiltshire Archaeological and Natural History Society, 2001), pp. 179–198.

Gannon, A., *The Iconography of Early Anglo-Saxon Coinage: Sixth to Eighth Centuries* (Oxford: Oxford University Press, 2003).

Gardner, K., 'The Wansdyke Dikat?' *Bristol and Avon Archaeology*, 15 (1998), pp. 57–65.

Gardner, K., 'The Land of Cyngar the Priest', in A. F. Smith (ed.), L. Fry, K. Gardner (assistant eds.), *The Last of the Britons -Kings, Thugs or Saints? Somerset and* adjoining counties, 400–700 AD. Papers from the Symposium held at Taunton 2005 (Taunton: CBA– South-West and SANHS, 2009), pp. 42–52.

Garmonsway, G. N. (ed. and transl.), *The Anglo-Saxon Chronicle* (London: J. M. Dent & Sons Ltd, 1972).

Gelling, M., *Place names in the Landscape* (London: J. M. Dent & Sons, 1984).

Geoffrey of Monmouth, *The History of the Kings of Britain*, L. Thorpe (transl.), (Harlow: Penguin, 1966).

Gerard, J., 'The End of Roman Bath', *Current Archaeology*, 217, Vol.XIX, no. 1 (April 2008), pp. 24–31.

Gover, J. E. B., A. Mawer, F. M. Stenton, *The Place names of Wiltshire, English Place name Society volume XVI* (Nottingham: English Place name Society, 1939).

Gretsch, M., *The Intellectual Foundations of the English Benedictine Reform* (Cambridge: Cambridge University Press, 1999).

Grierson, P., M. Blackburn, *Medieval European Coinage: The Early Middle Ages, 5th–10th centuries* (Cambridge: Cambridge University Press, 1986).

Grinsell, L. V., *The Bristol Mint: an Historical Outline* (Bristol: Historical Association, Bristol Branch, 1972).

Grinsell, L. V., *The History and Coinage of the Bristol Mint* (Bristol: City of Bristol Museum and Art Gallery, 1986).

Grundy, G. B., 'The Saxon land charters of Wiltshire', *Archaeological Journal*, volume 77 (1920), pp. 8–126.

Grundy, G. B., *The Saxon Charters and Field Names of Somerset* (Taunton: Somersetshire Archaeological and Natural History Society, 1935).

Grundy, G. B., 'The Ancient Woodland of Wiltshire', *Wiltshire Archaeological and Natural History Magazine*, XXXLVIII (1939), pp. 530–598.

Halsall, G., *Worlds of Arthur* (Oxford: Oxford University Press, 2013).

Hare, M., 'Anglo-Saxon Berkeley: History and Topography', *Anglo-Saxon Studies in Archaeology and History*, 18 (2013), pp. 119–156.

Harrison, K., *The Framework of Anglo-Saxon History: To A.D. 900* (Cambridge: Cambridge University Press, 2010).

Harvey, R. B., 'Shaftesbury Abbey's 12th century Rentals for Bradford on Avon', *Wiltshire Archaeological and Natural History Magazine*, 91 (1998), pp. 76–89.

Haslam, J., *Anglo-Saxon Towns in Southern England* (Chichester: Phillimore, 1984).

Haslam, J, 'King Alfred and the Vikings: Strategies and Tactics 876–886 AD', *Anglo-Saxon Studies in Archaeology and History*, 13 (2005), pp. 122–154.

Haslam, J., 'Daws Castle, Somerset, and civil defence measures in southern and midland England in the ninth to eleventh centuries', *Archaeological Journal*, 168 (2011), pp. 195– 226.

Higham, N. J., D. H. Hill (eds.), *Edward the Elder: 899–924* (Abingdon: Routledge, 2001).

Hill, D., *An Atlas of Anglo-Saxon England* (Oxford: Blackwell, 1981).

Hinton, D. A., 'Recent Work at the Chapel of St Laurence, Bradford on Avon, Wiltshire', *The Archaeological Journal*, 166 (2009), pp. 193–209.

Hobbs, R., *British Iron Age Coins in the British Museum* (London: British Museum Press, 1996).

Hooke, D., *The Anglo-Saxon Landscape: The Kingdom of the Hwicce* (Manchester: Manchester University Press, 1985).

John, E., *Reassessing Anglo-Saxon England* (Manchester: Manchester University Press, 1996).

Jones, M., *The End of Roman Britain* (Ithaca: Cornell University Press, 1996).

Jones, M., 'Cities and Urban Life', in M. Todd (ed.), *A Companion to Roman Britain* (Oxford: Blackwell 2004), pp. 162–192.

Jorgensen, A. (ed.), *Reading the Anglo-Saxon Chronicle: Language, Literature, History* (Turnhout: Brepols, 2010).

Karkov, C., *The Ruler Portraits of Anglo-Saxon England* (Woodbridge: Boydell Press, 2004).

Kelly, S. E. (ed.), *Charters of Shaftesbury Abbey, Anglo-Saxon Charters V* (Oxford: Oxford University Press/British Academy, 1996).

Kelly, S.E. (ed.), *Charters of Malmesbury Abbey, Anglo-Saxon Charters 11* (Oxford: Oxford University Press, 2005).

Kelly, S. E. (ed.), *Charters of Bath and Wells, Anglo-Saxon Charters 13* (Oxford: Oxford University Press, 2007).

Kemble, J. M., *Codex Diplomaticus Aevi Saxonici*, 6 vols. (London: Sumptibus Societatis, 1839-48).

Keynes, S., M. Lapidge (transl.), *Alfred the Great. Asser's Life of King Alfred and other contemporary Sources* (Harmondsworth: Penguin, 1983).

Kirby, D. P., *The Earliest English Kings* (Abingdon: Routledge, 2000).

Koch, J., *Celtic Culture: a Historical Encyclopedia* (Santa Barbara: ABC-CLIO, 2006).

Lambdin, L.C., R.T. Lambdin (eds.), *Encyclopedia of Medieval Literature* (Abingdon: Routledge, 2013).

Lapidge, M., J. Blair, S. Keynes, *The Blackwell Encyclopaedia of Anglo-Saxon England* (Oxford: Blackwell, 1999).

Lapidge, M., M. Herren (eds.), *Aldhelm: The Prose Works* (Cambridge: Cambridge University Press, 1979).

Lavelle, R., *Aethelred II: King of the English 978-1016* (Stroud: Tempus, 2002).

Lavelle, R., *Alfred's Wars: Sources and Interpretations of Anglo-Saxon Warfare in the Viking Age* (Woodbridge: Boydell Press, 2010).

Laycock, S., 'Buckles and Bosnia. Britannia, the Threat Within', *British Archaeology*, number 87 (March/April, 2006), pp. 10–15.

Laycock, S., *Britannia the Failed State* (Stroud: Tempus, 2008).

Laycock, S., *Warlords: The Struggle for Power in Post-Roman Britain* (Stroud: The History Press, 2009a).

Laycock, S., 'Buckles, Belts and Borders: How Soldiers' Fashions Reflect Political Turmoil in Late Roman Britain', *Current Archaeology*, 20, no.6 (2009b), pp. 12–19.

Leech, R. H. 'The medieval defences of Bristol revisited', in L. Keen (ed.), *'Almost the Richest City': Bristol in the Middle Ages* (London: British Archaeological Association Conference Transaction, vol 19, 1997), pp. 18–30.

Leins, I., 'What can be Inferred from the Regional Stylistic Diversity of Iron Age coinage?', in D. Garrow, C. Gosden, J. D. Hill (eds.), *Rethinking Celtic Art* (Oxford: Oxbow Books, 2008), pp. 100–112.

Lyon, S., 'The coinage of Edward the Elder', in N. J. Higham and D. H. Hill (eds.), *Edward the Elder: 899–924* (Abingdon: Routledge, 2001), pp. 67–78.

Magennis, H., M. Swan, *A Companion to Ælfric* (Leiden: Brill, 2009).

Marsden, R., *The Cambridge Old English Reader* (Cambridge: Cambridge University Press, 2004).

Matthew Paris, *Chronica Majora*, H.R.Luard (ed.) *Matthæi Parisiensis, Monachi Sancti Albani, Chronica Majora* (London: Rolls Series, 1872–83).

Mattingly, D., *An Imperial Possession* (Harlow: Allen Lane, 2006).

Myres, J. N. L., *The English Settlements* (Oxford: Oxford University Press, 1986).

Nash, D. *Coinage in the Celtic World* (London: Spink & Son Ltd, 1987).

North, J. J., *English Hammered Coinage, Volume 1: Early Anglo-Saxon to Henry III, c. 600-1272* (London: Spink & Son Ltd, 1994).

Ó Floinn, R., 'Patrons and Politics: Art, Artefact and Methodology', in M. Redknap, N. Edwards, S. Youngs, A. Lane, J. Knight (eds.), *Pattern and Purpose in Insular Art* (Oxford: Oxbow Books, 2001), pp. 1–14.

O'Leary, T. J., 'Excavations at Upper Borough Walls, Bath', *Medieval Archaeology*, XXV (1981), pp. 1–30.

Papworth, M., *Deconstructing the Durotriges. A Definition of Iron Age Communities within the Dorset Environs, British Archaeological Reports, British Series 462* (Oxford: Archaeopress, 2008).

Papworth, M., *The Search for the Durotriges* (Stroud: The History Press, 2011).

Plunkett, S. J., 'Mercian and West Saxon Decorative Stone-Sculpture: Schools, Styles and Patterns of Influence' (unpubl. PhD thesis, 2 vols., Cambridge University, 1984).

Ponsford, M. W., *Bristol Castle: Archaeology and the History of a Royal Fortress* (M. Litt thesis, 1979, Bristol Library).

Rackham, O., *Trees and Woodland in the British Landscape* (London: J. M. Dent & Sons, 1976).

Rahtz, P., *The Saxon and Medieval Palaces at Cheddar* (Oxford: BAR, British Series, 1979).

Rahtz, P., 'The Dobunnic Area in post-Roman times', in M. Ecclestone, N. Holbrook, A. Smith (eds.), *The Land of the Dobunni: a Series of Papers Relating to the Transformation of the Pagan, Pre-Roman, Tribal Lands into Christian, Anglo-Saxon Gloucestershire and Somerset* (Great Dunham: Heritage Marketing and Publications Ltd, 2003), pp. 24–31.

Reynolds, A., 'The Early Medieval Period', in N. Holbrook, and J. Jurica (eds.), *Twenty five years of Archaeology in Gloucestershire: A Review of New Discoveries and New Thinking in Gloucestershire, South Gloucestershire and Bristol 1979-2004, Bristol and Gloucestershire Archaeology Report No.3* (Cirencester: Cotswold Archaeology, 2006), pp. 141–160.

Reynolds, A., A. Langlands, 'Social Identities on the Macro Scale a Maximum View of Wansdyke', in W. Davies, G. Halsall, A. Reynolds (eds.), *People and Space in the Middle Ages 300–1300, Studies in the Early Middle Ages 28* (Turnhout: Brepols, 2007), pp. 13–37.

Rivet, A. L. F., C. Smith, *The Place-names of Roman Britain* (London: B. T. Batsford Ltd, 1979).

Round, J. H., 'The third penny', *English Historical Review*, vol. 34 (1919), pp. 62–64.

Salway, P., *Roman Britain* (Oxford: Oxford University Press, 1981).

Schoenfeld, E. J., 'Anglo-Saxon *Burhs* and Continental *Burgen*: Early Medieval Fortifications in Constitutional Perspective', *The Haskins Society Journal*, 6 (1994), pp. 49–66.

Sims-Williams, P., *Religion and Literature in Western England 600-800* (Cambridge: Cambridge University Press, 1990).

Sims-Williams, P., 'The Settlement of England in Bede and the Chronicle', *Anglo-Saxon England*, Volume 12 (1983), pp. 1–41.

Slotkin, E., 'The Fabula, Story and Text of Breuddwyd Rhonabwy', *Cambridge Medieval Celtic Studies*, Issue 18, University of Cambridge, Department of Anglo-Saxon, Norse and Celtic (1989), pp. 89–111.

Stenton, F., *Anglo-Saxon England* (Oxford: Oxford University Press, 1943).

Symonds, M., 'Corinium's Dead: Excavating the Tetbury Road Roman Cemetery', *Current Archaeology*, Issue 281 (August 2013), pp. 28–34.

Thormann, J., 'The Anglo-Saxon Chronicle Poems', in A. J. Frantzen, J. D. Niles (eds.), *Anglo-Saxonism and the Construction of Social Identity* (Gainesville: University Press of Florida, 1997), pp. 60–85 .

Thorn, C., F. Thorn (eds. and transl.), *Domesday Book: Wiltshire* (Chichester: Phillimore, 1979).

Todd, M., *Roman Britain* (Oxford: Blackwell 1999).

Webster, G., *The Roman Invasion of Britain* (Abingdon: Routledge, 2003).

White, R., Britannia Prima (Stroud: Tempus, 2007).

Whitelock, D. (ed.), *English Historical Documents, Volume I, c. 500–1042* (London: Eyre Methuen, 1979).

Whitelock, D., D. C. Douglas, S. I. Tucker (transl. and eds.), *The Anglo-Saxon Chronicle* (London: Eyre and Spottiswoode, 1961).

Whittock, H., 'Why does the north-western boundary of Wiltshire ignore the river Avon?' *The Wiltshire Archaeological and Natural History Magazine*, volume 105 (2012), pp. 96–104.

Whittock, H., 'The Annexation of Bath by Wessex: the Evidence of Two Rare Coins of Edward the Elder', *British Numismatic Journal*, volume 82 (2012), pp. 46–53.

Whittock, M., 'Reflections on the cultural context and function of the West Wansdyke', *Bristol and Avon Archaeology*, 7 (1988), pp. 2–5.

Whittock, M., *A Brief History of Life in the Middle Ages* (London: Constable and Robinson, 2009).

Wickham, C., *Framing the Early Middle Ages* (Oxford: Oxford University Press, 2005).

William of Malmesbury, *Gesta Pontificvm Anglorvm* (*The History of the English Bishops*), volume one, M. Winterbottom (ed. and transl.) with the assistance of R. M. Thomson, (Oxford: Oxford University Press, 2007).

William of Malmesbury, *Gesta Regum Anglorum: The History of the English Kings*, *vol. I*, R. A. B. Mynors, (ed. and transl., completed by R. M. Thomson, M. Winterbottom), (Oxford: Oxford University Press, 1998).

William of Malmesbury, *The Deeds of the Bishops of England* (*Gesta Pontificum Anglorum*), D. Preest (transl.), (Woodbridge: Boydell Press, 2002).

William of Malmesbury, *Vita S. Dunstani*, in M. Winterbottom and R. M. Thomson (eds. and transl.), *William of Malmesbury, Saints' Lives* (Oxford: Oxford Medieval Texts, 2002), pp. 166–303.

Williams, A., *Kingship and Government in Pre-Conquest England, c. 500–1066* (Basingstoke: Palgrave Macmillan, 1999).

Williams, A., G. H. Martin (eds.), *Domesday Book: a Complete Translation* (Harlow: Penguin, 2003).

Williamson, T., *Sutton Hoo and its Landscape: The Context of Monuments* (Oxford: Windgather Press, 2008).

Yorke, B., *Kings and Kingdoms of Early Anglo-Saxon England* (London: B. A. Seaby Ltd, 1990).

Yorke, B., *Wessex in the Early Middle Ages* (London: Leicester University Press, 1995).

Yorkston, D. E., *Archaeological Evaluation at Rodway Hill Sports ground, Pomphrey Hill Road, Mangotsfield* (2008). Report held by South Gloucestershire council.

Author Biographies

Hannah Whittock was raised in Bradford on Avon (Wiltshire) and attended St Laurence School (named from the 'Saxon Church' in the town). She graduated with a 'First' in Anglo-Saxon, Norse and Celtic from Pembroke College, Cambridge University, in 2011. In 2012 she completed her MPhil at Cambridge, researching the relationship of the Bradford on Avon charter of 1001 to the development of the cult of Edward King and Martyr. She is currently working with the devolved Welsh Government. Her publications include: 'Why does the north-western boundary of Wiltshire ignore the River Avon?', in *The Wiltshire Archaeological and Natural History Magazine*, vol. 105 (2012); 'The annexation of Bath by Wessex: The evidence of two rare coins of Edward the Elder', in *The British Numismatic Journal*, vol. 82 (2012); and *The Viking Blitzkrieg, 789–1098* (2013), co-authored with her father, Martyn Whittock. *The Anglo-Saxon Avon Valley Frontier* arises from her second year university dissertation on this subject and also from her MPhil dissertation, both carried out within the department of Anglo-Saxon, Norse and Celtic at Cambridge University, and also draws on her research into the Wiltshire county boundary and the annexation of Bath.

Martyn Whittock was born in Keynsham (Somerset), in the valley of the Avon, and graduated in politics from Bristol University in 1980 and since then has taught history at secondary level for over thirty years. He currently teaches history at a Wiltshire secondary school, where he is curriculum leader for Spiritual, Moral, Social and Cultural development. At A-Level his specialist subject is Late Roman Britain and Anglo-Saxon England, *c.* 350–1066. He is the author of forty school history textbooks and adult history books, the latter including: *A Brief History of Life in the Middle Ages* (2009), *A Brief History of the Third Reich* (2011), *The Viking Blitzkrieg, 789–1098* (2013), co-authored with his daughter Hannah Whittock, and *A Brief Guide to Celtic Myths and Legends* (2013). He is also the author of articles on the Anglo-

Saxon royal estate at Keynsham (north Somerset), the strategic significance of the West Wansdyke earthwork and, more recently, 'Medieval 'Signs and Marvels': insights into medieval ideas about nature and the cosmic order', *The Historian*, vol. 109 (The Historical Association, 2011). He has acted as an historical consultant to the National Trust and English Heritage. His role in the writing of *The Anglo-Saxon Avon Valley Frontier* has been collaborating with Hannah in bringing her research to book form and in developing the study further.